PHOTOGRAPHS OF THE BRITISH ISLES

The best travel selection

Tim Saunders

Tim Saunders Publications
tsaunderspubs.weebly.com

Copyright © 2022 Tim Saunders

All rights reserved

No part of this book may be reproduced, or stored in a retrieval system, or transmitted in any form or by any means, electronic, mechanical, photocopying, recording, or otherwise, without express written permission of the publisher.

Cover photograph: Suffolk cloudscape by Tim Saunders

To my family for their love, support and patience

It takes a lot of imagination to be a good photographer. You need less imagination to be a painter because you can invent things. But in photography everything is so ordinary; it takes a lot of looking before you learn to see the extraordinary.

DAVID BAILEY

CONTENTS

Title Page
Copyright
Dedication
Epigraph
Foreword
Cheshire — 1
Cornwall — 3
Devon — 6
Dorset — 11
Hampshire — 13
Herefordshire — 23
Kent — 25
London — 27
Norfolk — 34
Suffolk — 36
Pembrokeshire — 38
Sark — 40
Sussex — 43
Wales — 46
Wiltshire — 50

Animals	52
Birds	57
Flowers	61
LIMITED EDITION PRINTS	69
Tim Saunders Publications	71

FOREWORD

This book, a celebration of the beautiful British Isles, features the best photographs that I have taken over the past decade as a travel writer. The idea came to me while writing *Family Staycations in the British Isles* (also available from Tim Saunders Publications). You won't find any writing in this book, just photographs - postcards from me to you. It's a great pictorial record of some stunning subject matter. A camera always accompanies me on my travels. It is a necessary piece of equipment for a journalist and provides an easy way of recording important, and sometimes special moments.

    So, how did I decide which photographs were good enough to include? With digital photography it is so easy to point and click, with little consideration for composition or lighting. Very little skill is required. Over the past 10 years I must have taken thousands of photographs. As my own harshest critic I have to admit that few are exceptional. For me a great photograph shouts at me in the same way that a work of art, poem or good story does. It has that innate ability of tugging at the heart strings, demanding your attention. A bit like a good story there has to be a strong angle and over time this eye for detail has, thankfully, developed. So, a good photograph will be created when light hits a carefully considered composition in just the right way. It's all subjective of course. I have enjoyed sifting through my portfolio, carefully making my selection.

Organised in alphabetical order by county, my favourite ones have to be the stunning cloudscapes in Suffolk, which really do stand out. For that reason one has been selected for the book cover. That said, Kent also provides great interest. There I have been able to take a very satisfying seascape. I also find myself drawn to structures like windmills, which have great historic value in the same way that fine architecture does. Fields, wildlife and insects always amaze me, too. When the light and the subject matter combine there really can be some exquisite results.

Every single part of the British Isles provides fabulous opportunities for the keen photographer but they do not all feature in this book, either because I have yet to visit them or my photographs were simply not good enough. In this book you will find the very best photographs that I have taken since 2012. The digital cameras I use are: Panasonic Lumix, Kodak and Akaso. I hope you enjoy browsing as much as I enjoyed taking them.

My photographs are available as limited edition prints here: https://www.artfinder.com/artist/tim-saunders

Tim Saunders
tasaunders.weebly.com

CHESHIRE

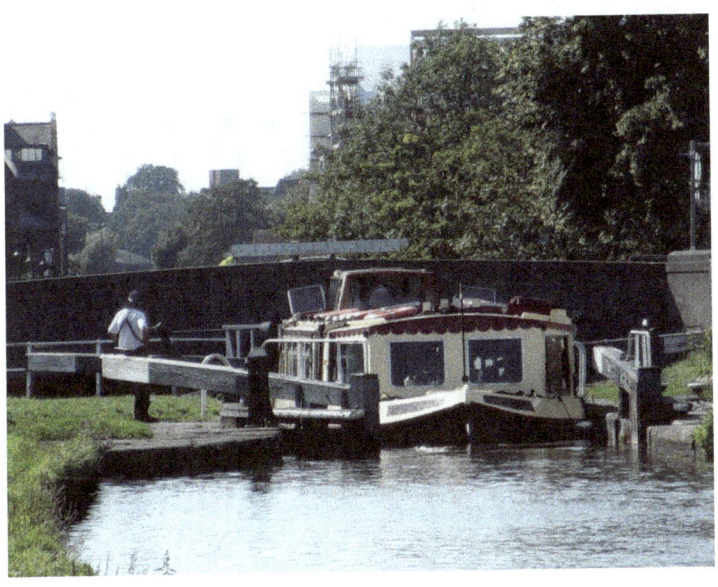

TIM SAUNDERS

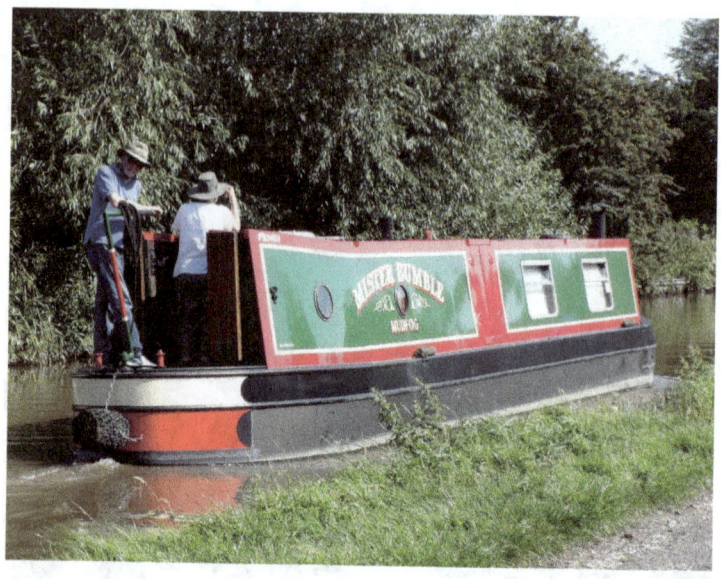

CORNWALL

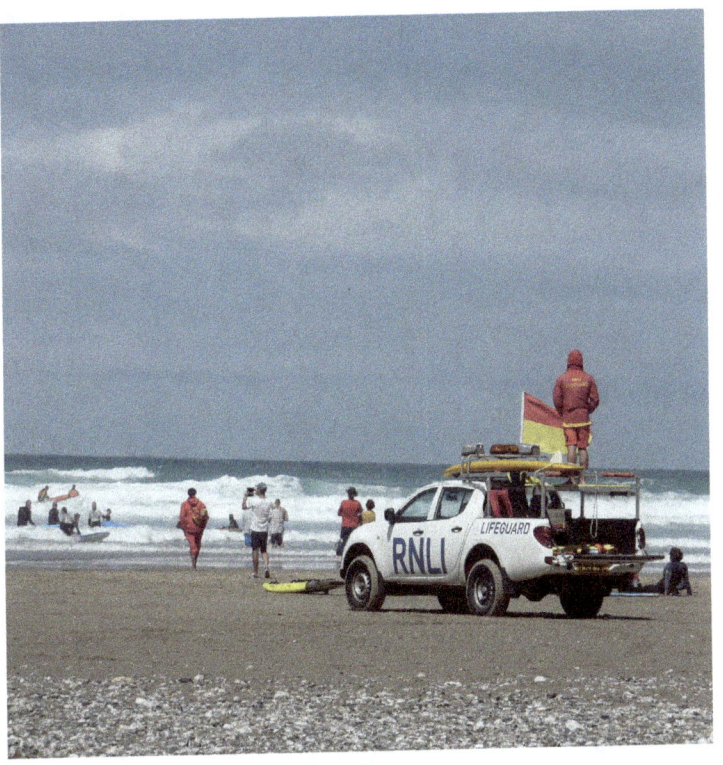

TIM SAUNDERS

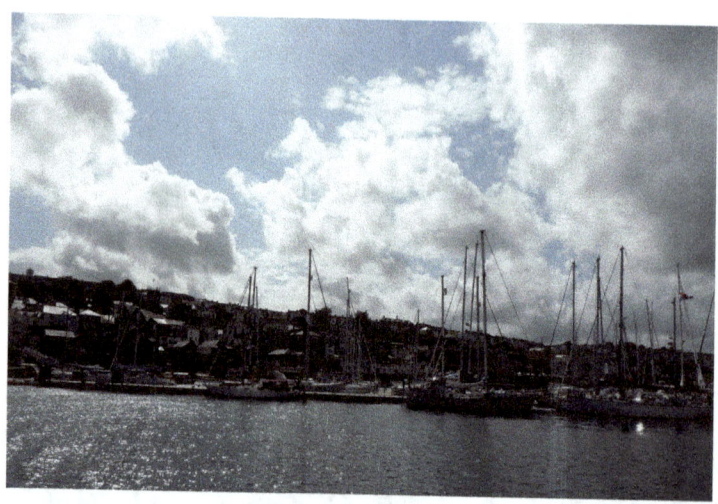

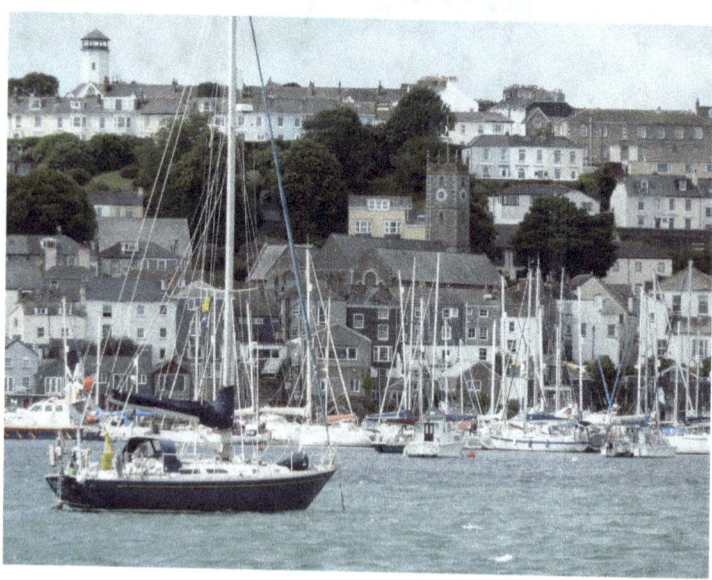

PHOTOGRAPHS OF THE BRITISH ISLES

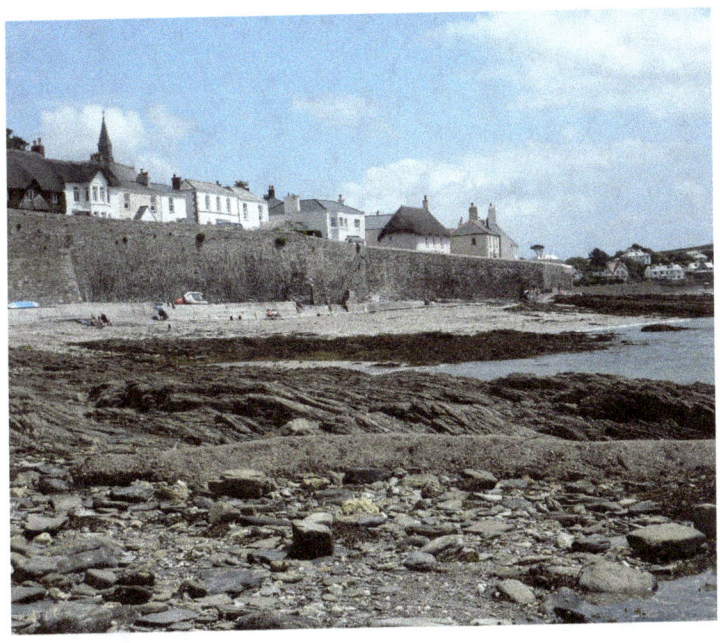

DEVON

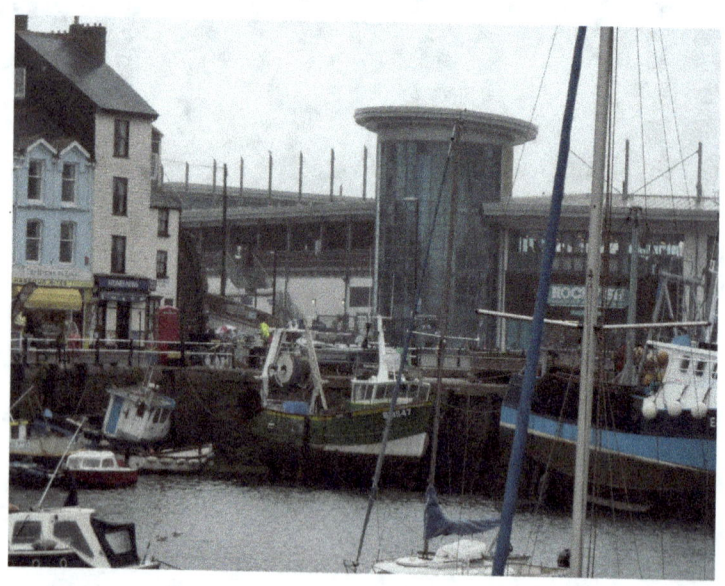

PHOTOGRAPHS OF THE BRITISH ISLES

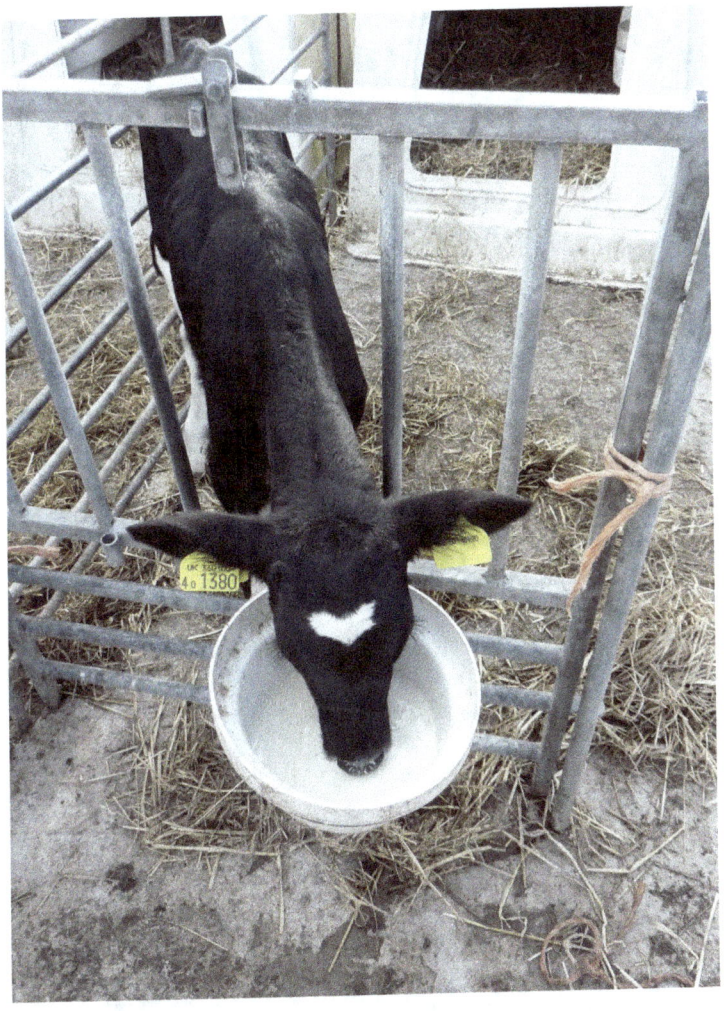

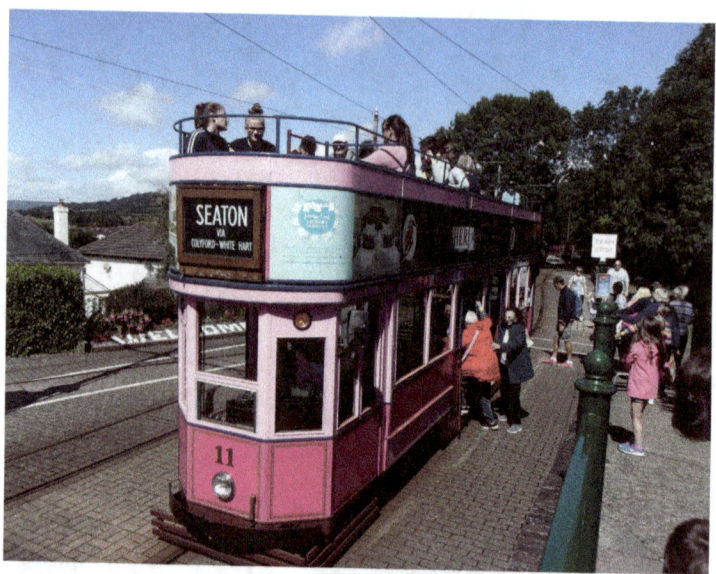

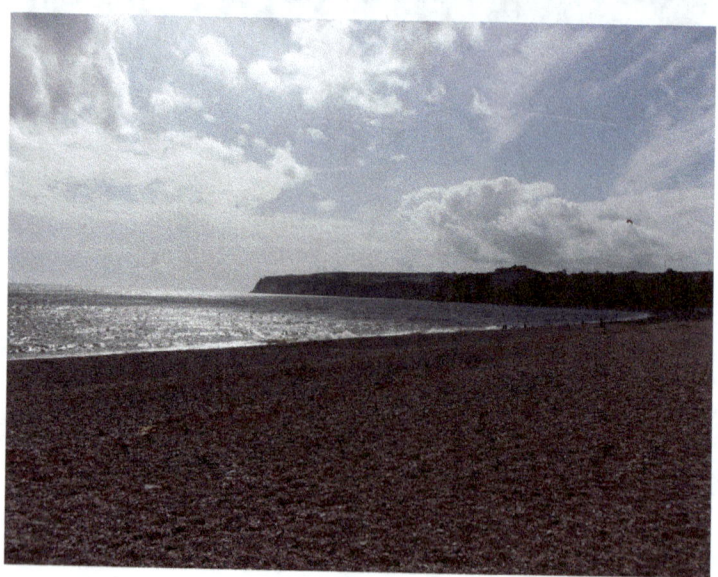

PHOTOGRAPHS OF THE BRITISH ISLES

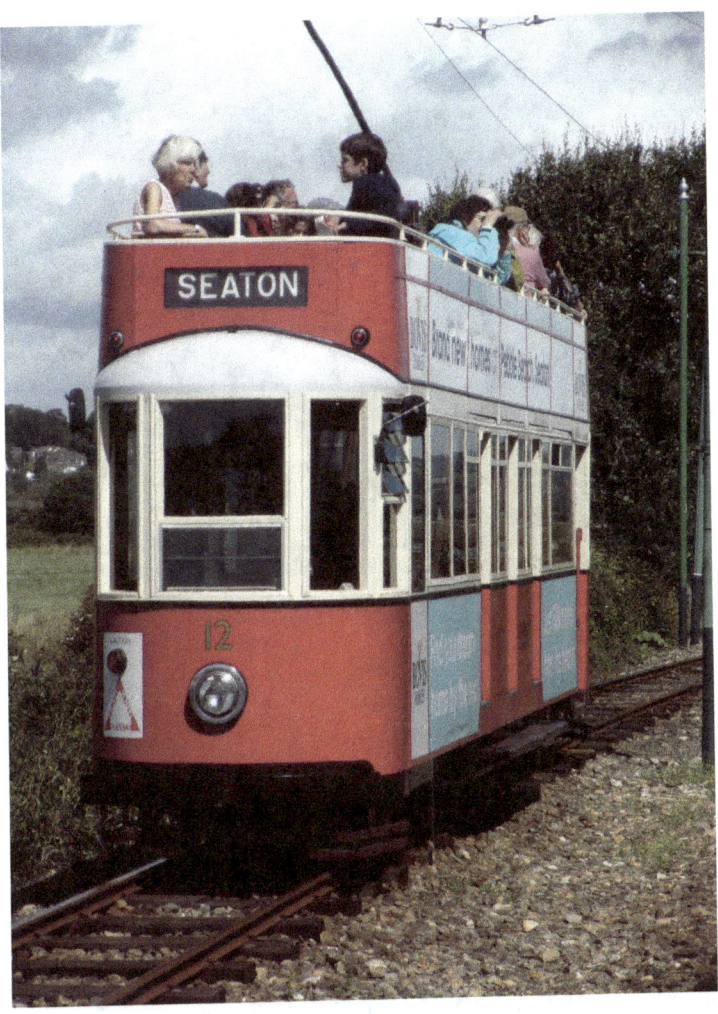

TIM SAUNDERS

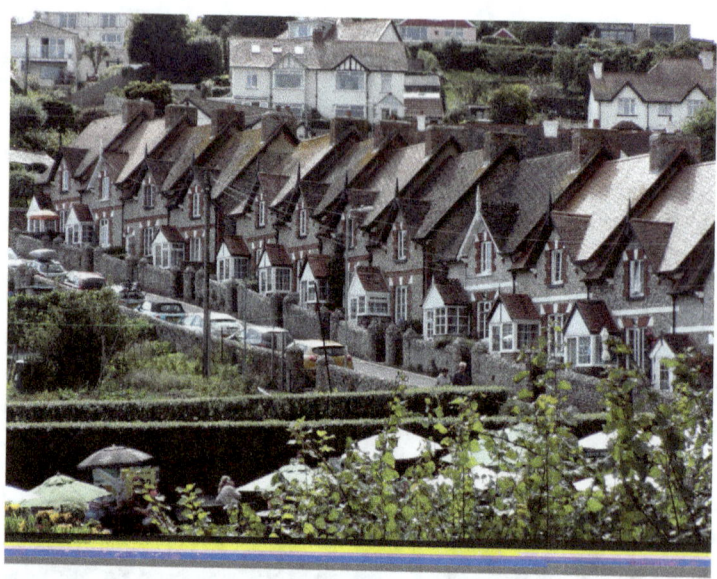

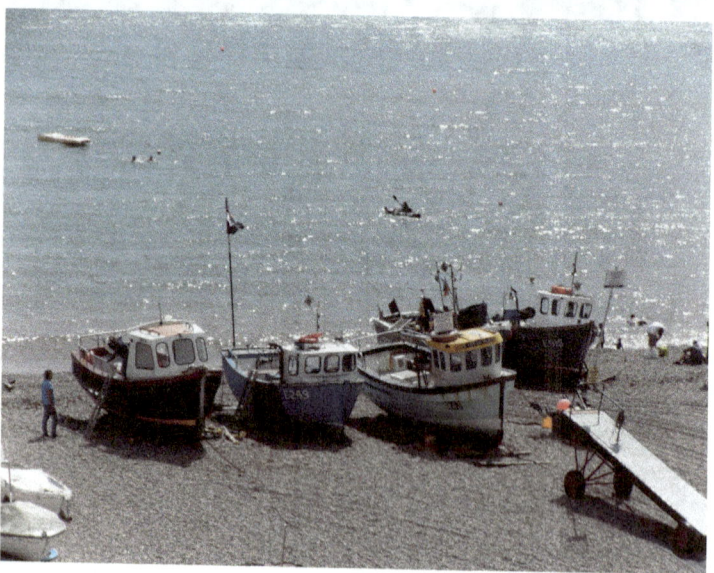

DORSET

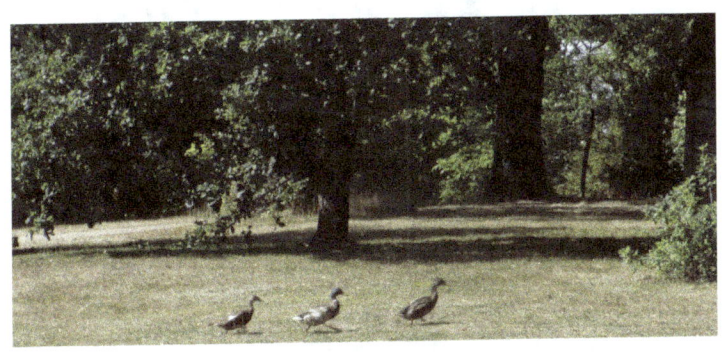

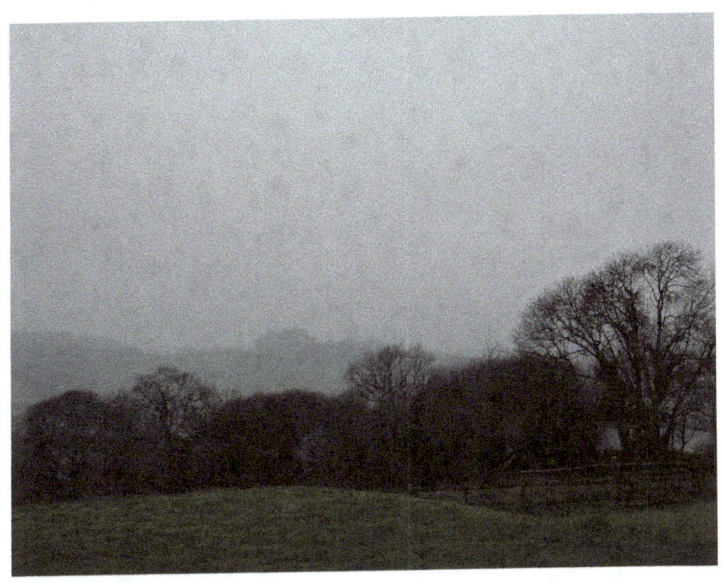

TIM SAUNDERS

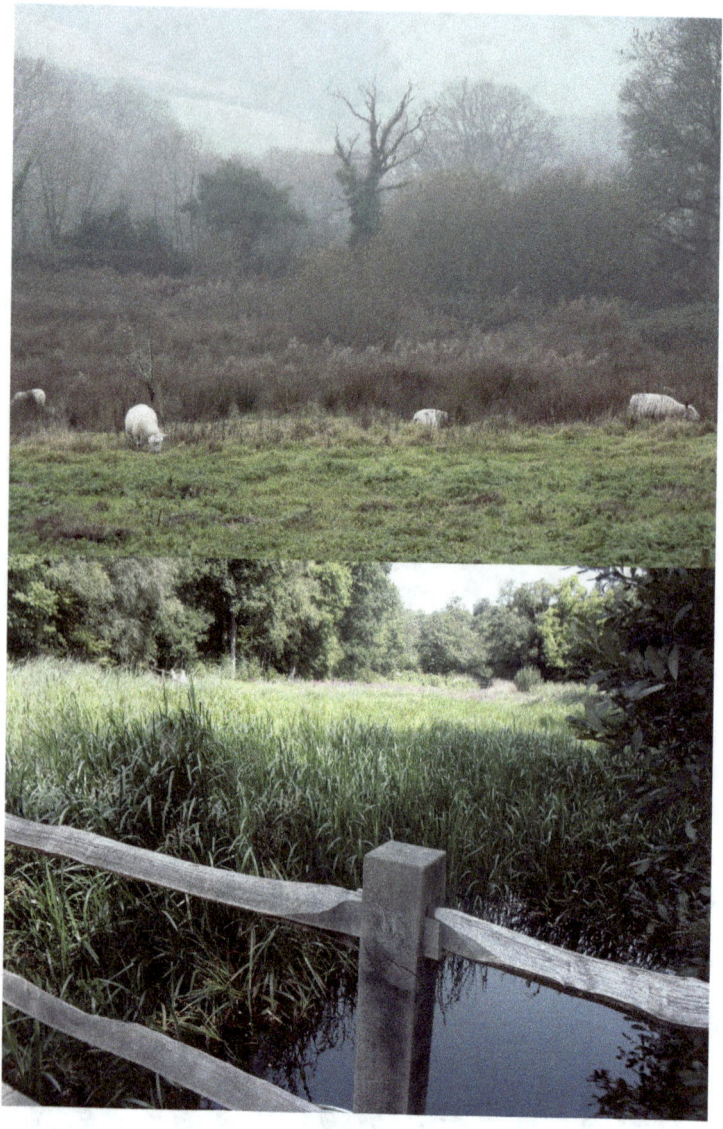

HAMPSHIRE
and the Isle of Wight

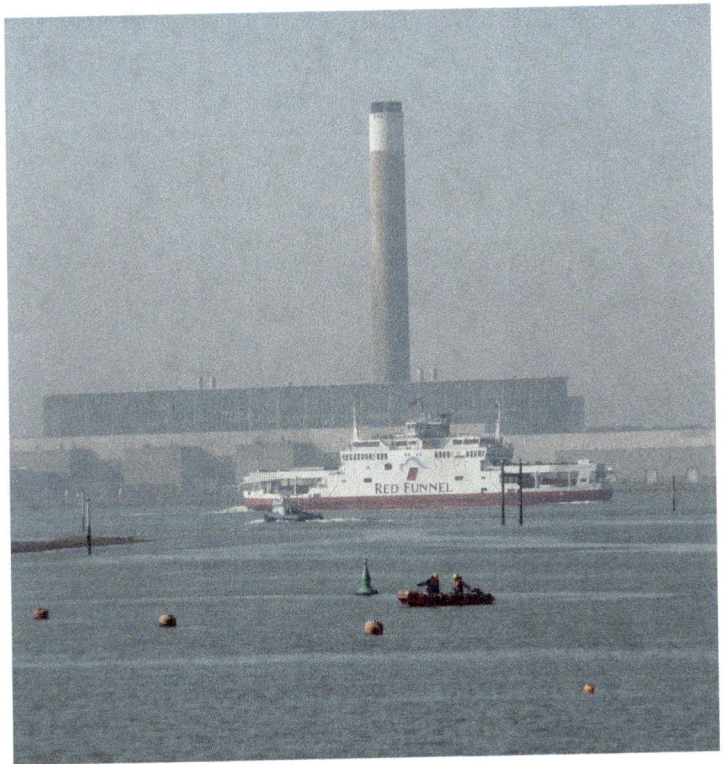

TIM SAUNDERS

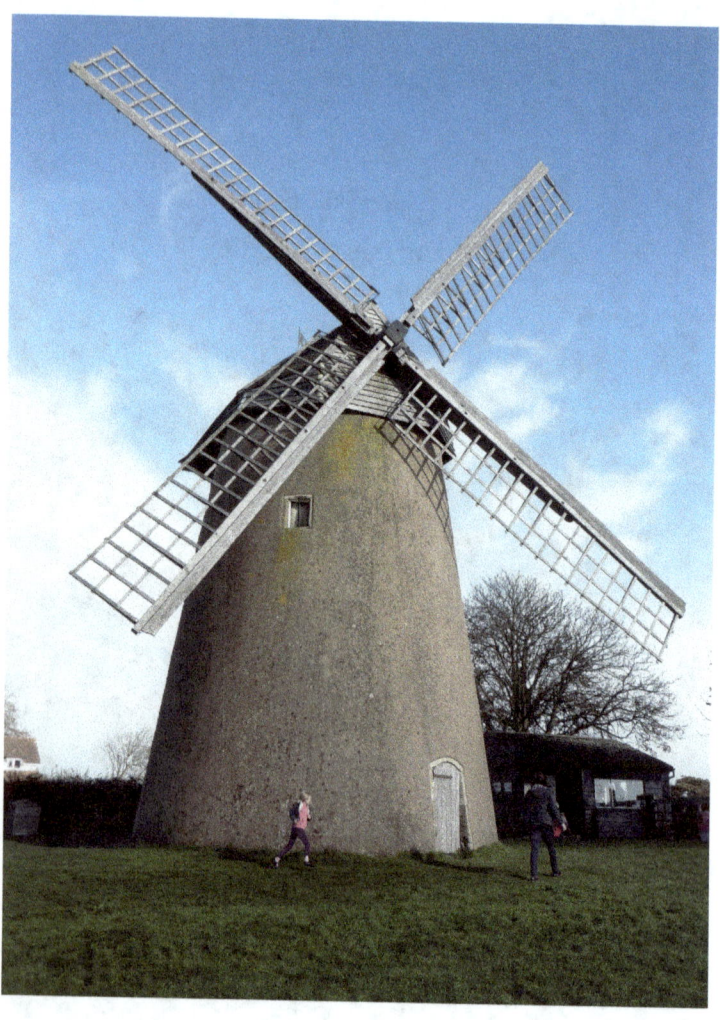

PHOTOGRAPHS OF THE BRITISH ISLES

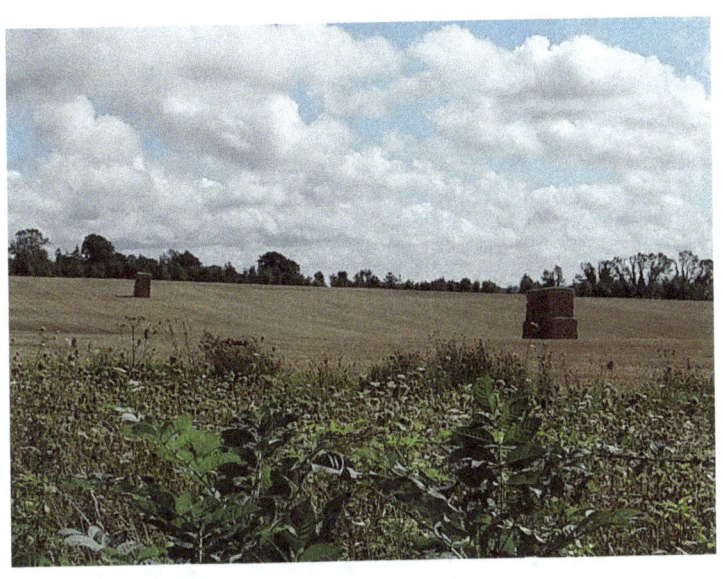

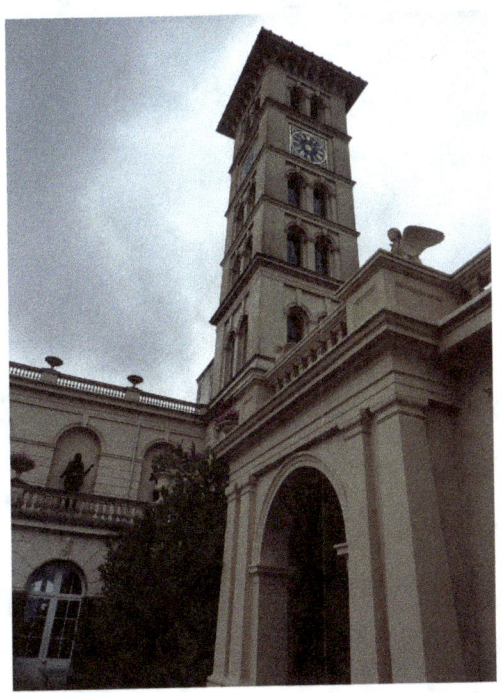

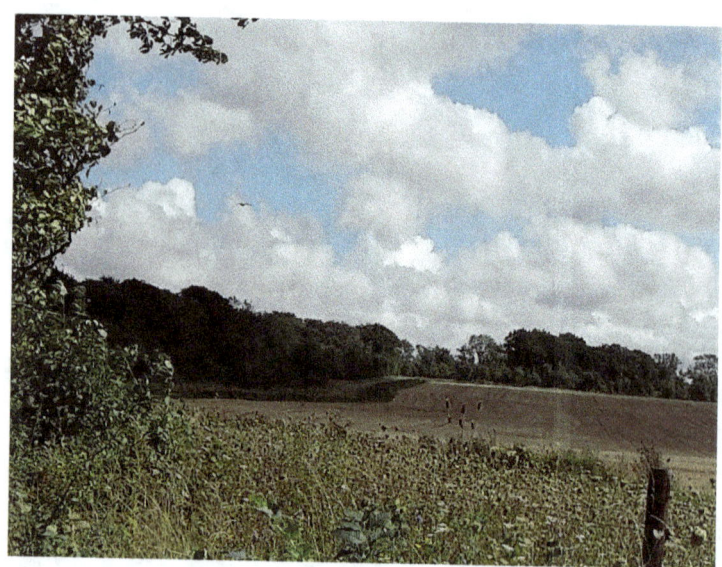

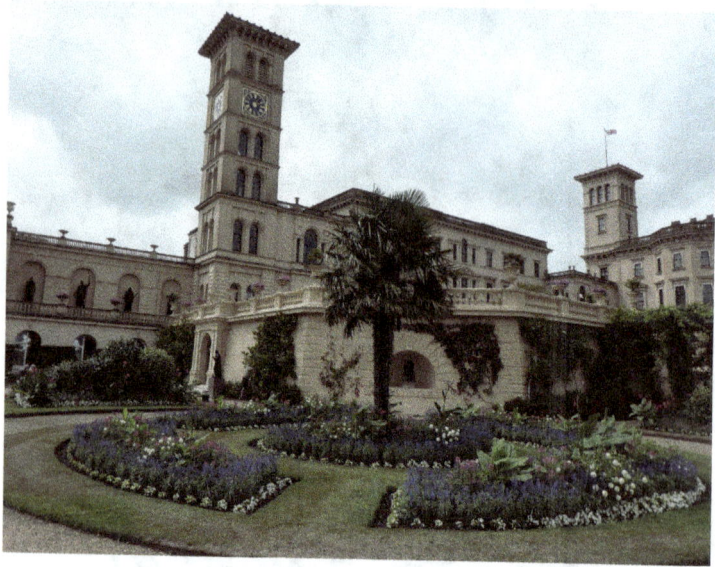

PHOTOGRAPHS OF THE BRITISH ISLES

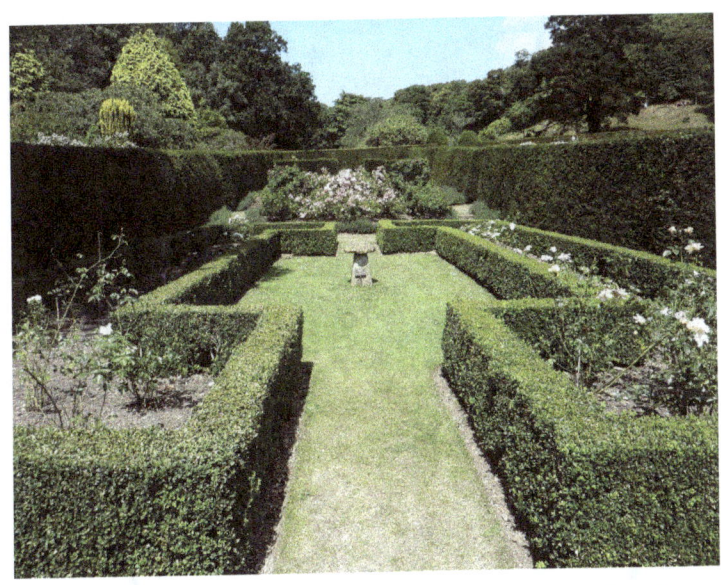

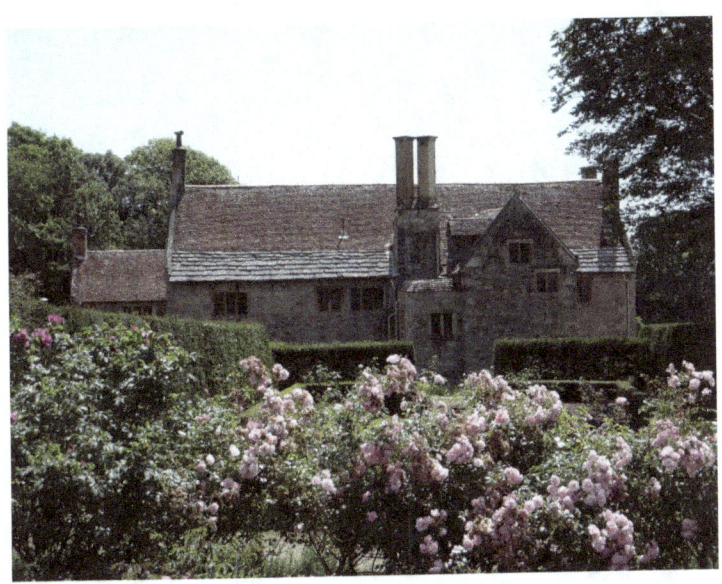

TIM SAUNDERS

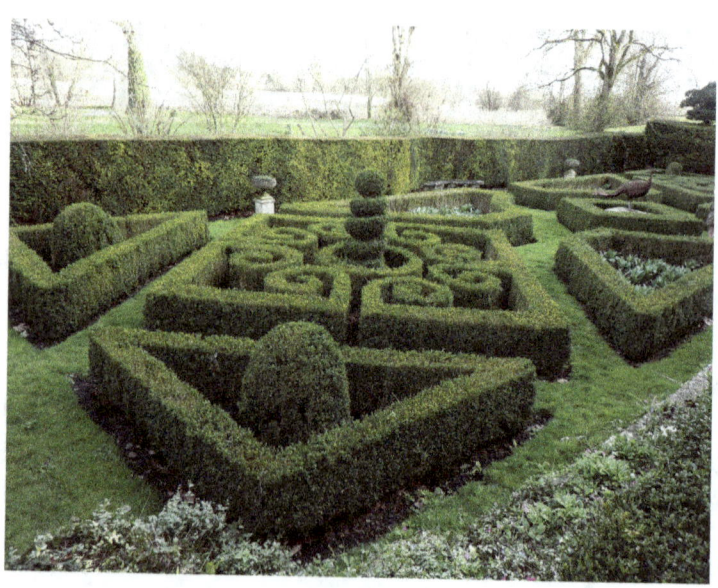

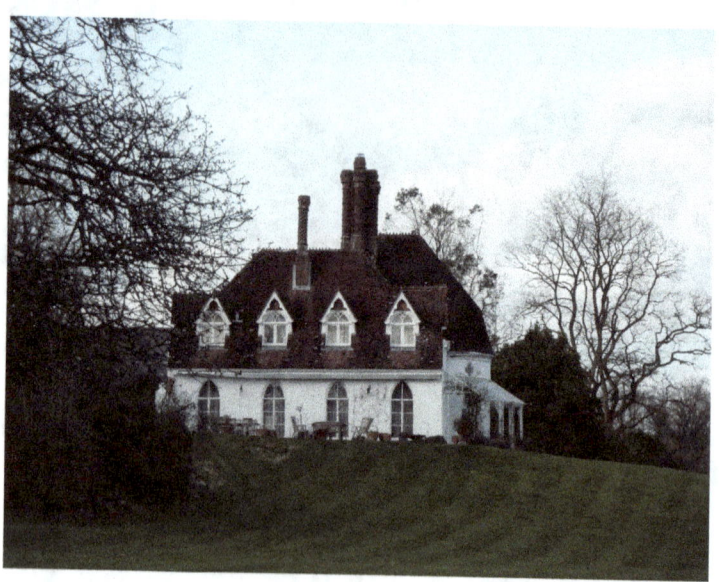

PHOTOGRAPHS OF THE BRITISH ISLES

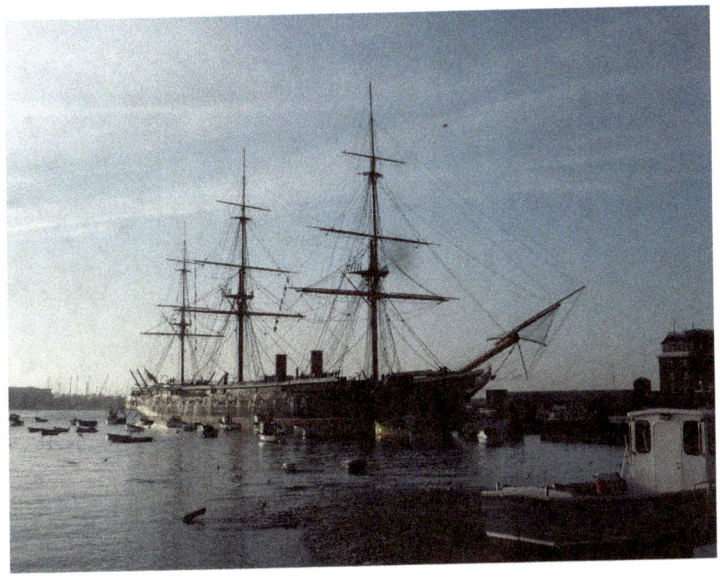

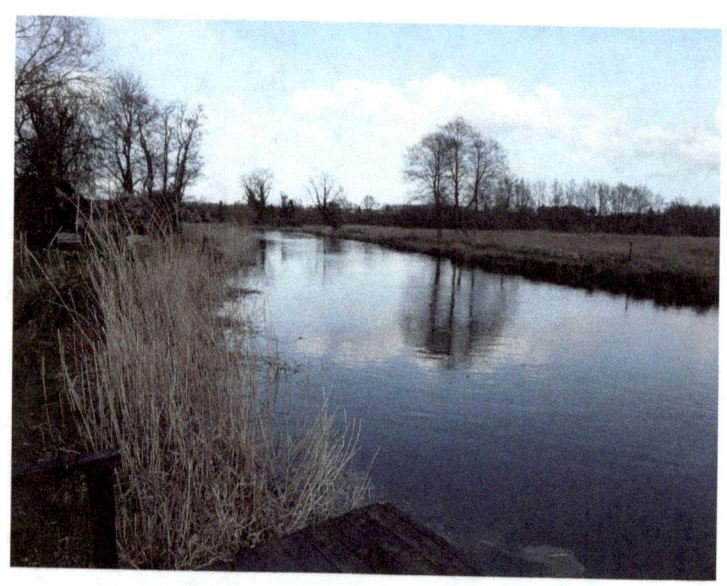

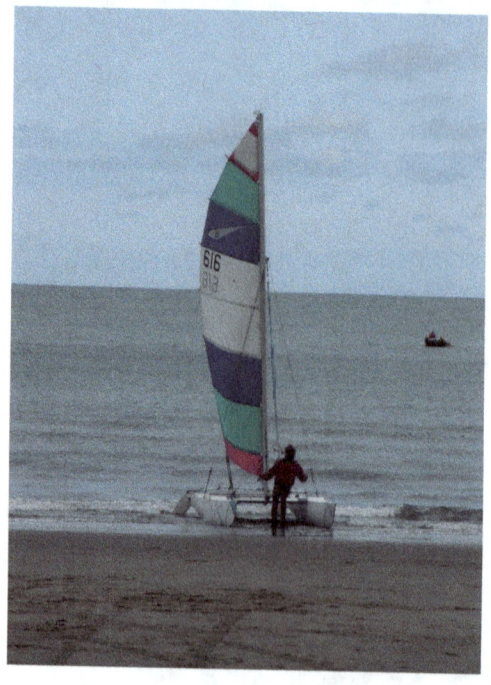

PHOTOGRAPHS OF THE BRITISH ISLES

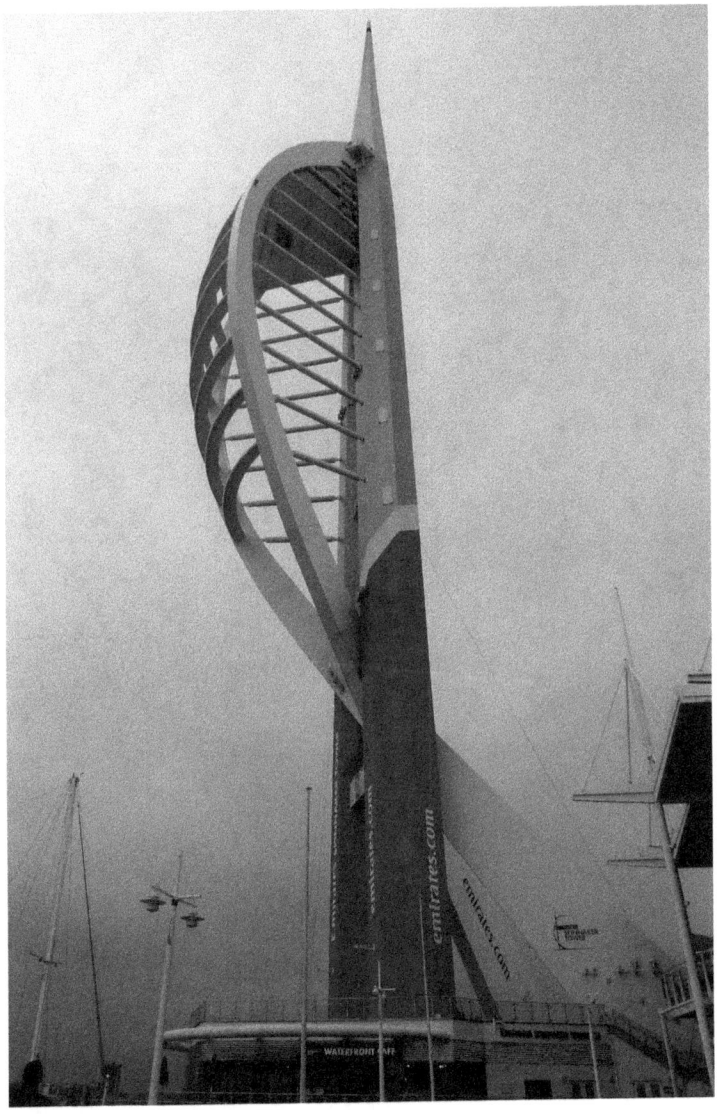

TIM SAUNDERS

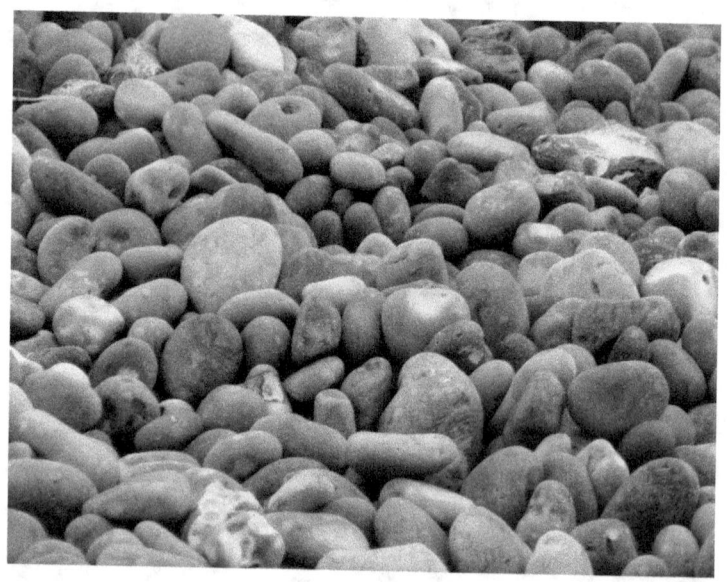

HEREFORDSHIRE

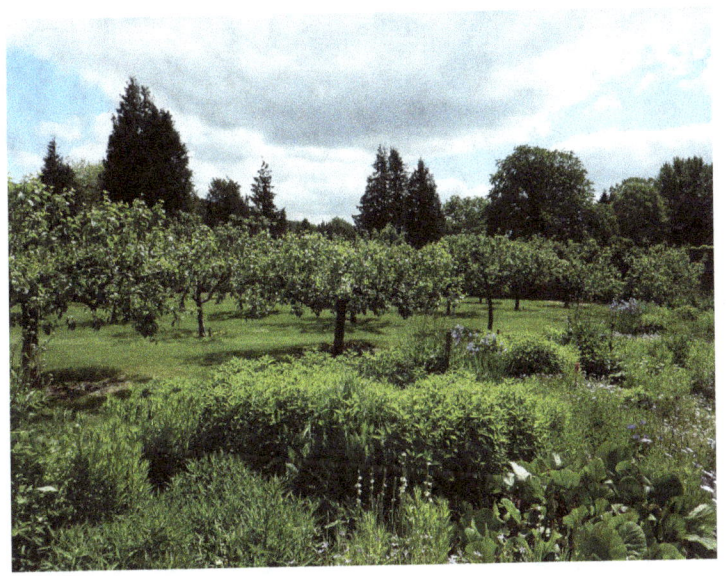

TIM SAUNDERS

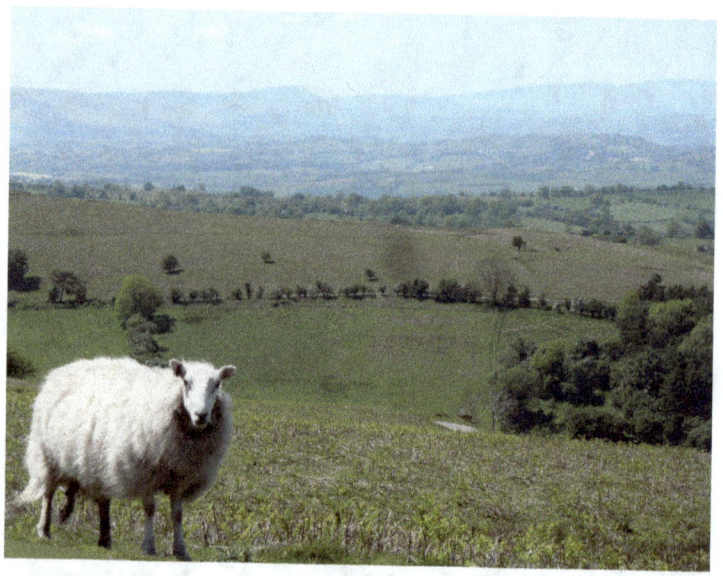

KENT

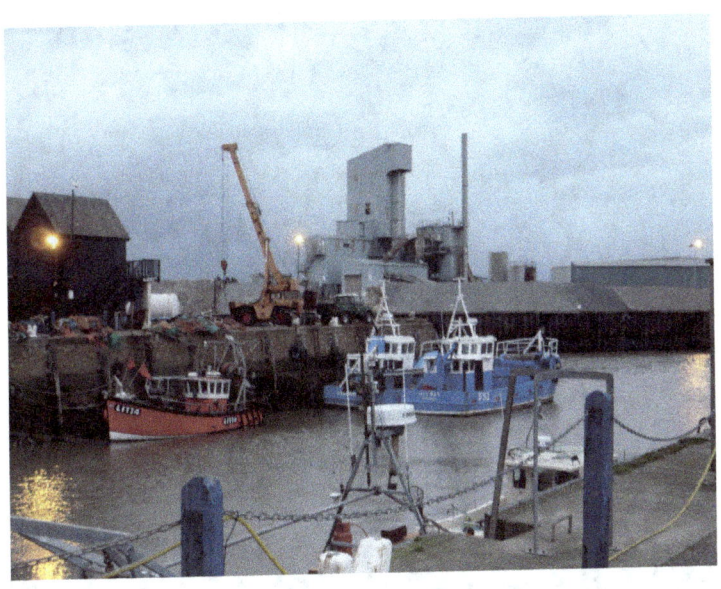

TIM SAUNDERS

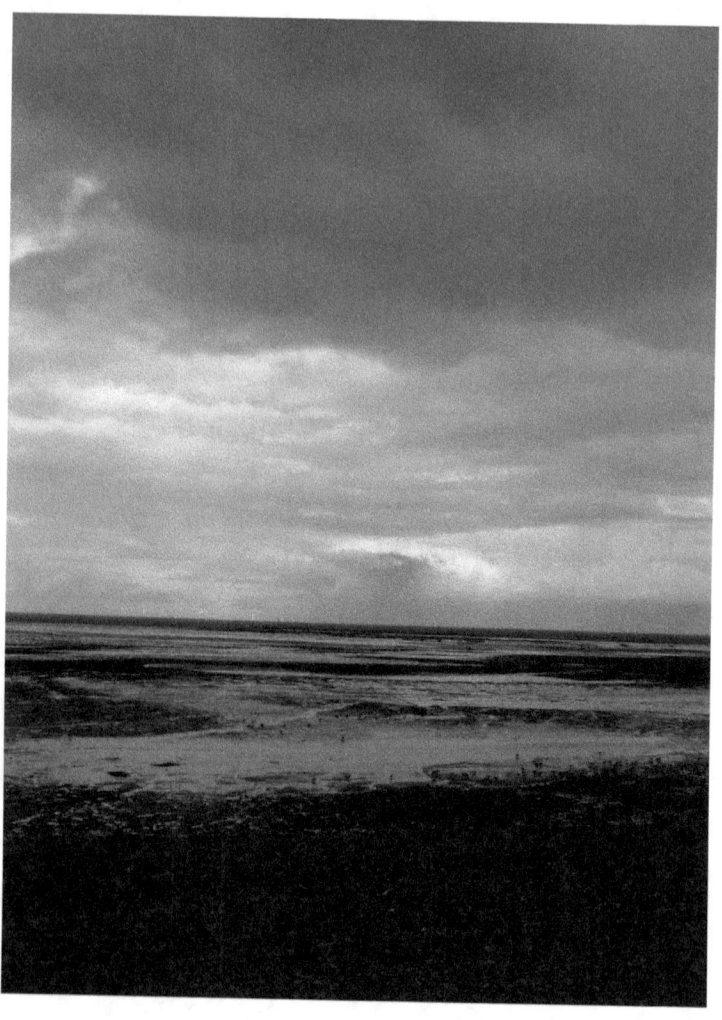

LONDON

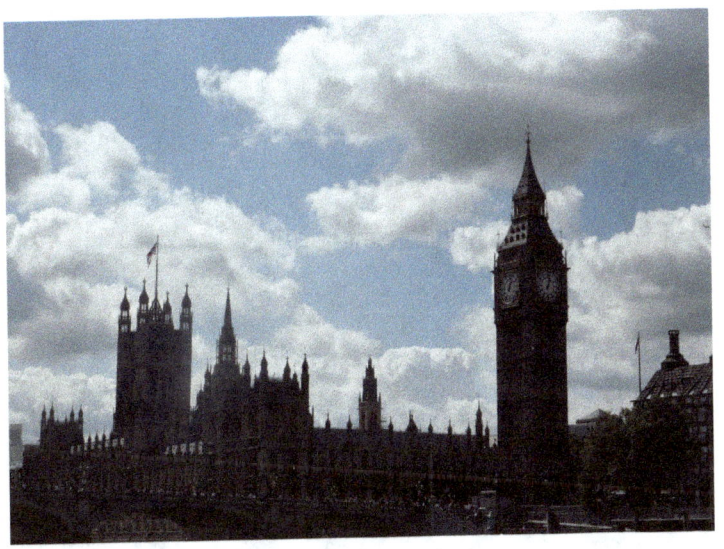

TIM SAUNDERS

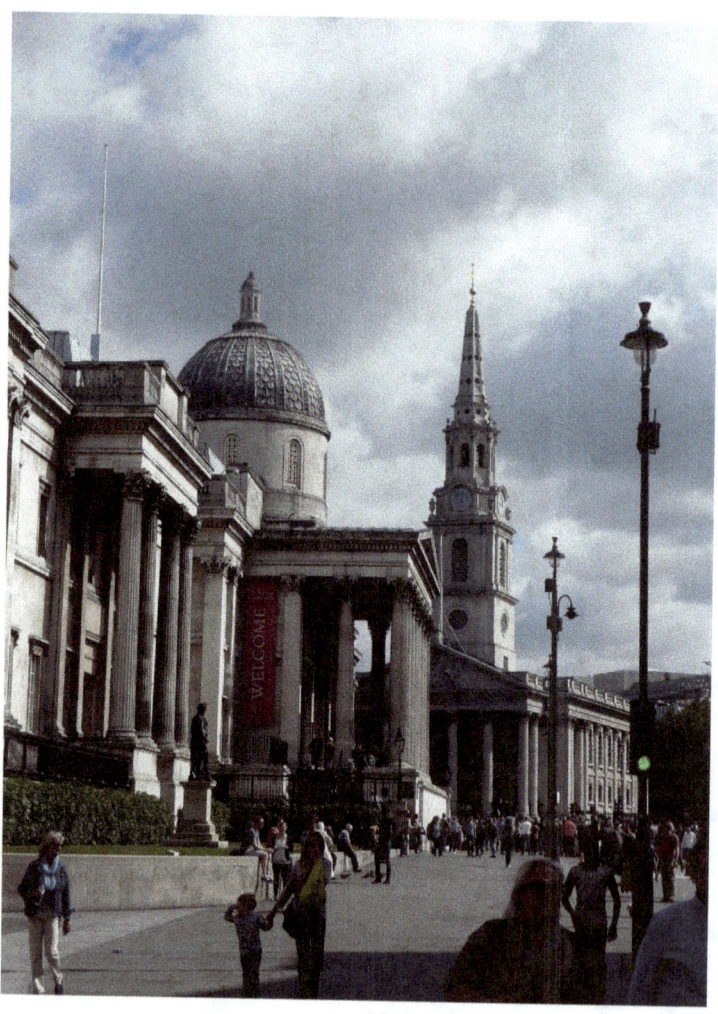

PHOTOGRAPHS OF THE BRITISH ISLES

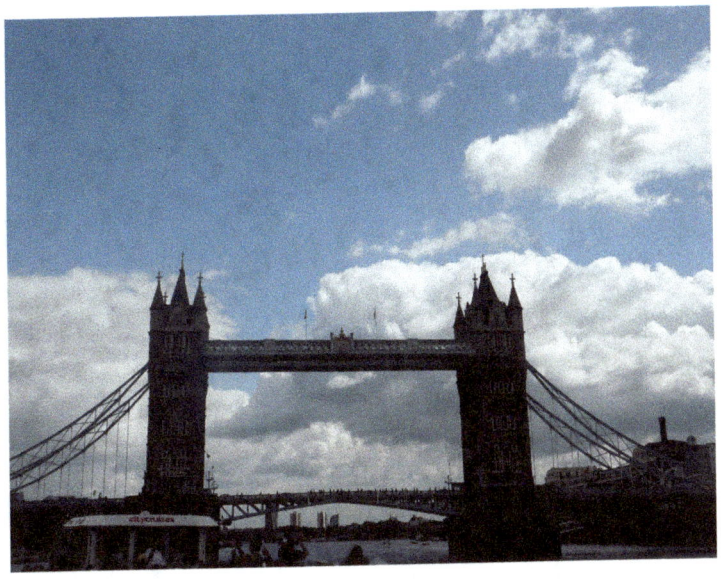

TIM SAUNDERS

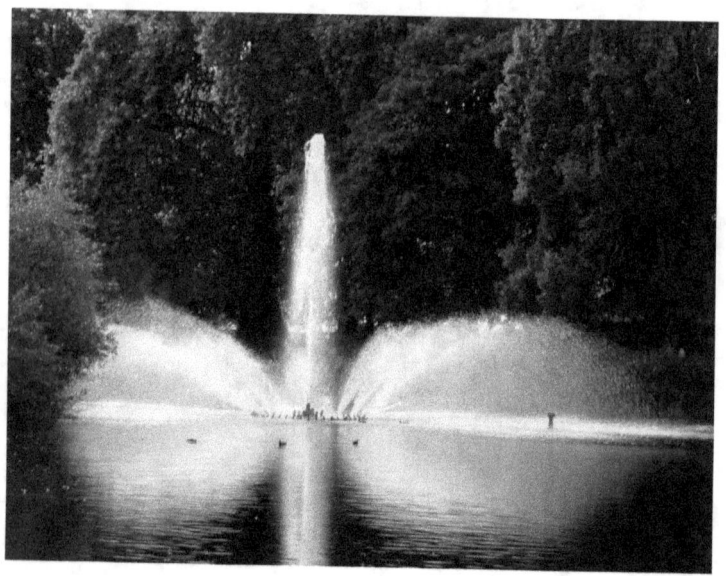

PHOTOGRAPHS OF THE BRITISH ISLES

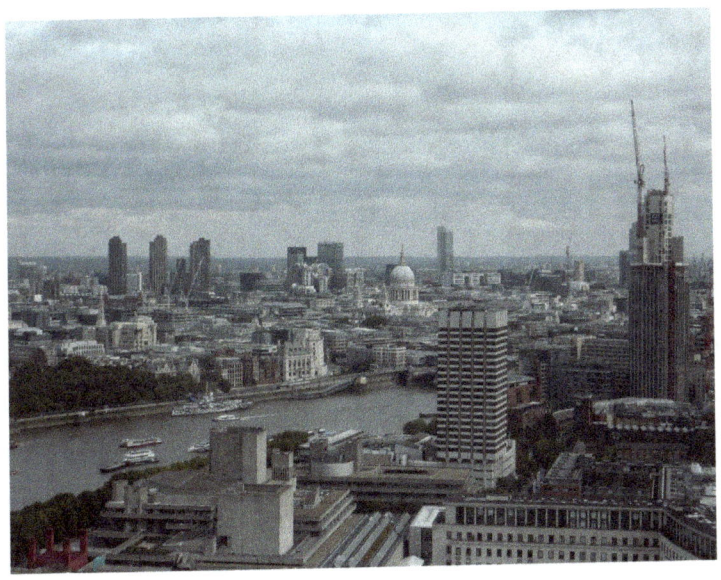

TIM SAUNDERS

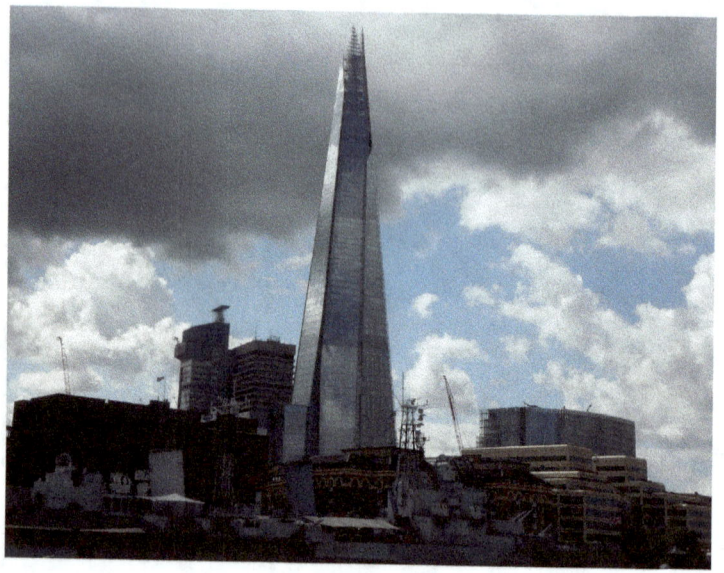

PHOTOGRAPHS OF THE BRITISH ISLES

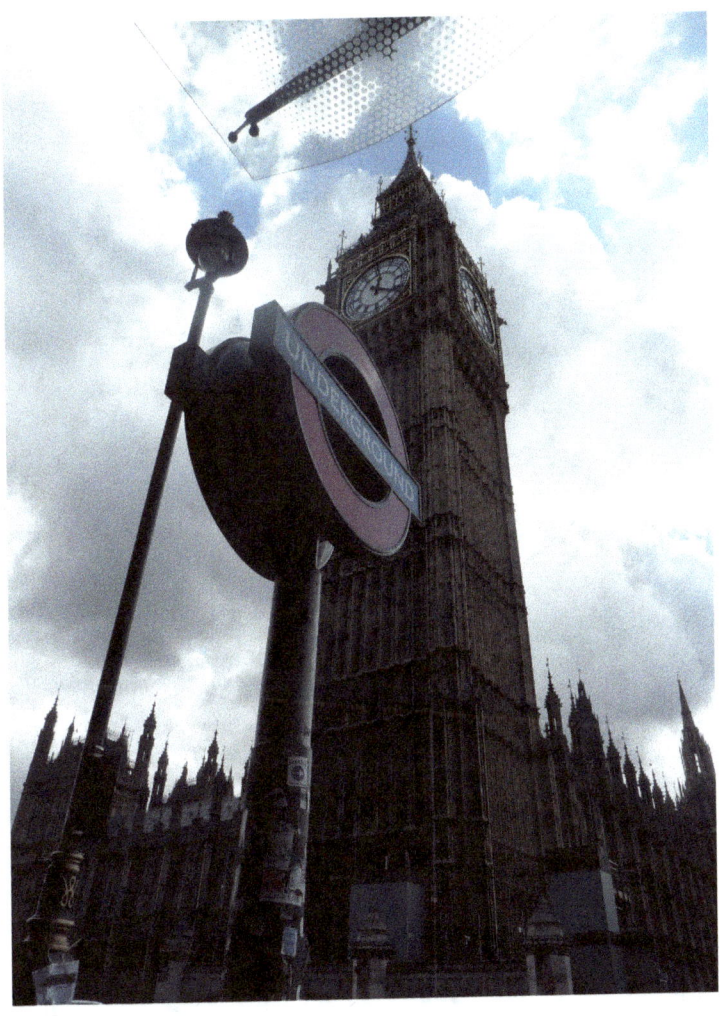

NORFOLK

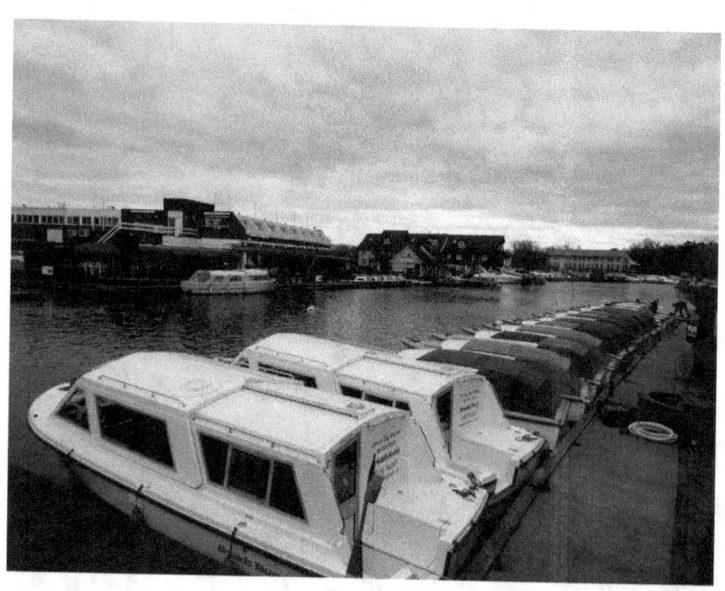

PHOTOGRAPHS OF THE BRITISH ISLES

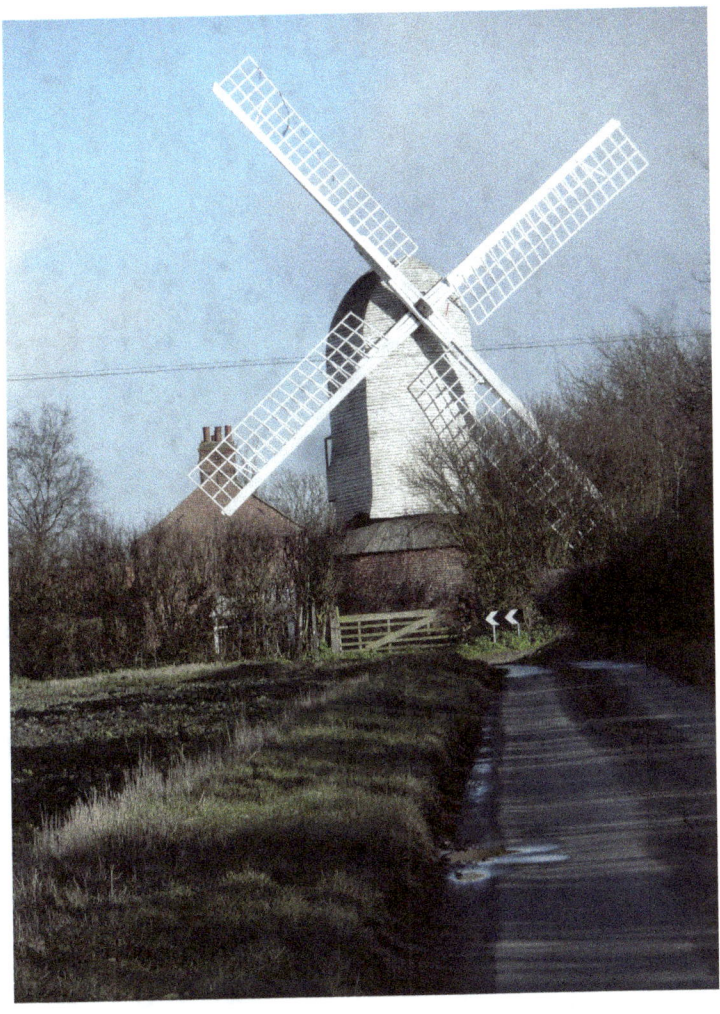

SUFFOLK

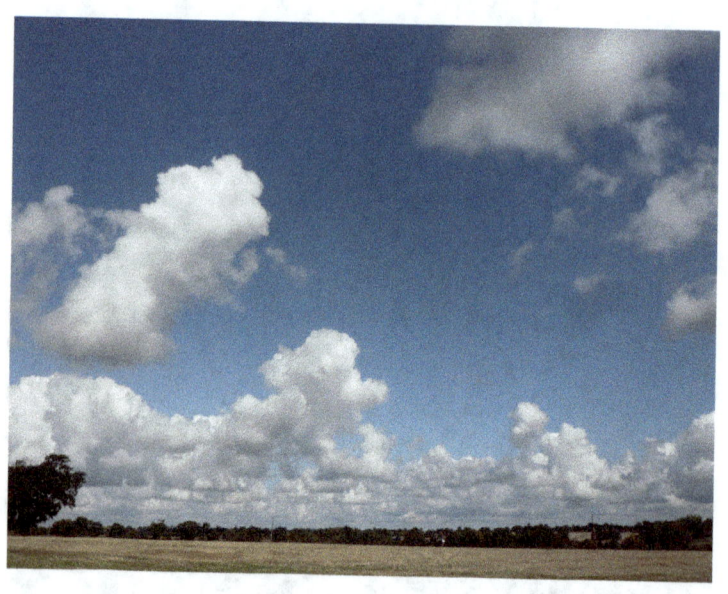

PHOTOGRAPHS OF THE BRITISH ISLES

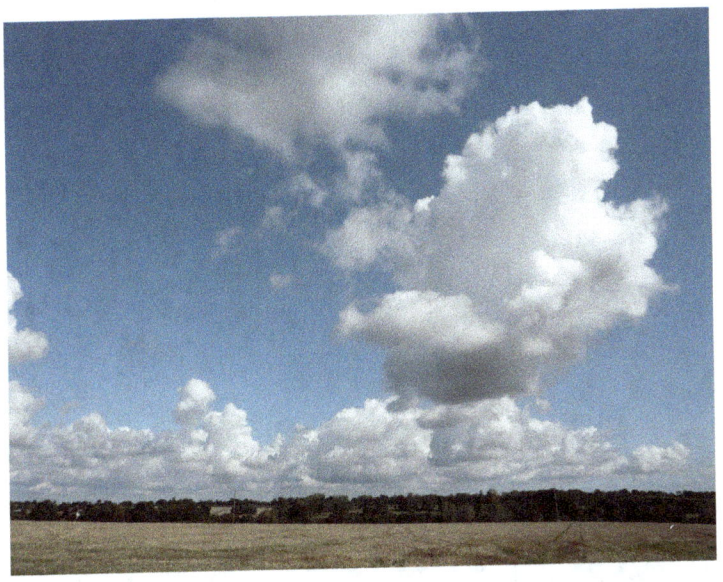

PEMBROKESHIRE

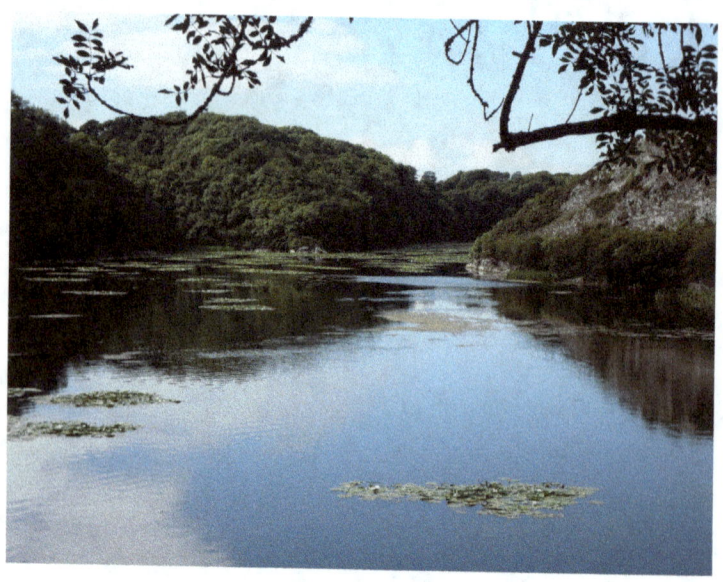

PHOTOGRAPHS OF THE BRITISH ISLES

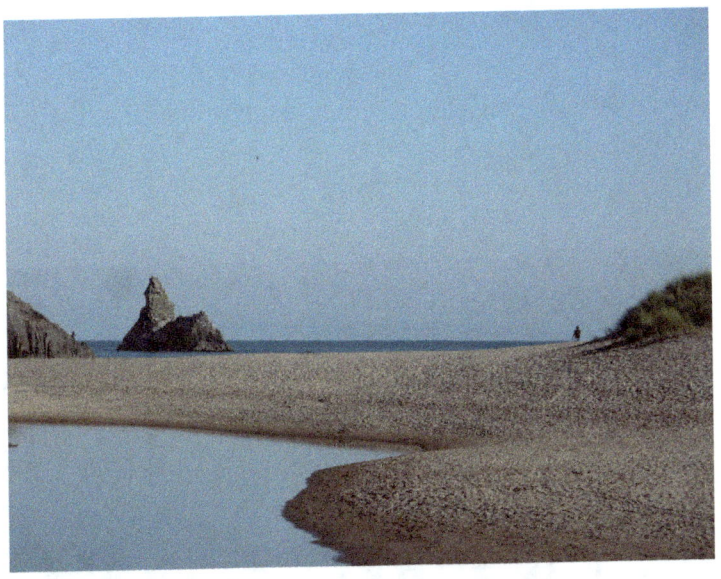

SARK

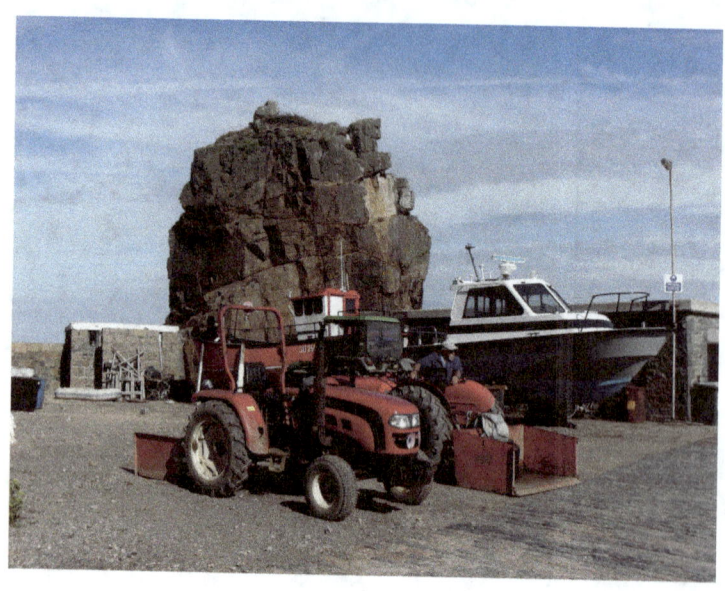

PHOTOGRAPHS OF THE BRITISH ISLES

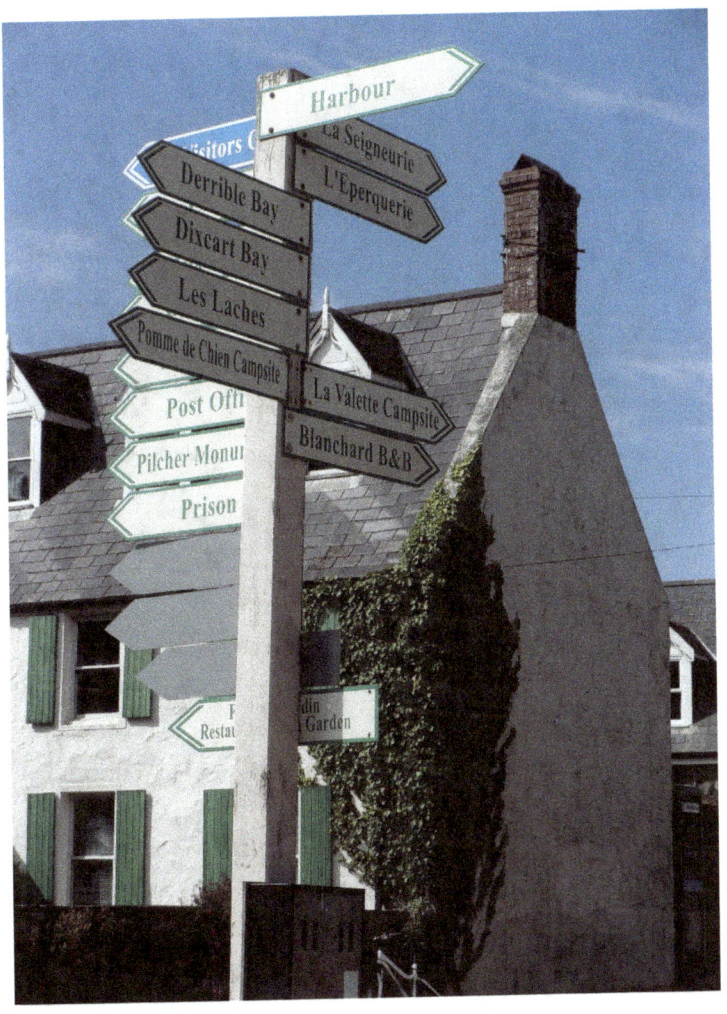

TIM SAUNDERS

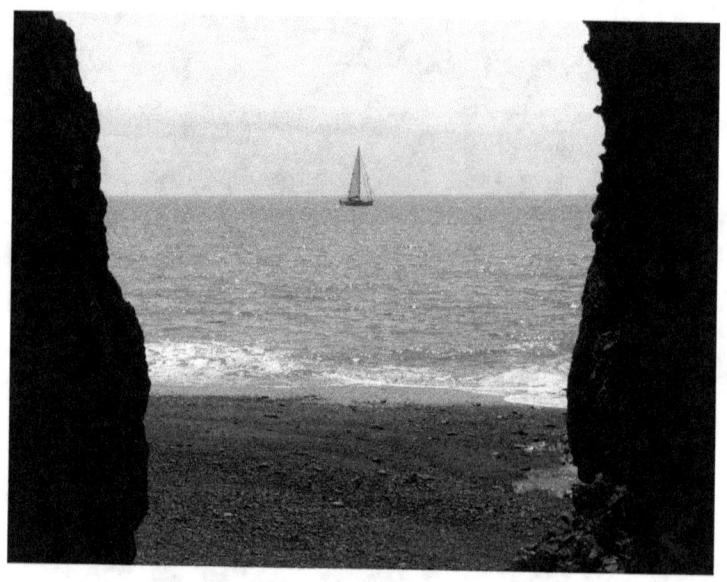

SUSSEX

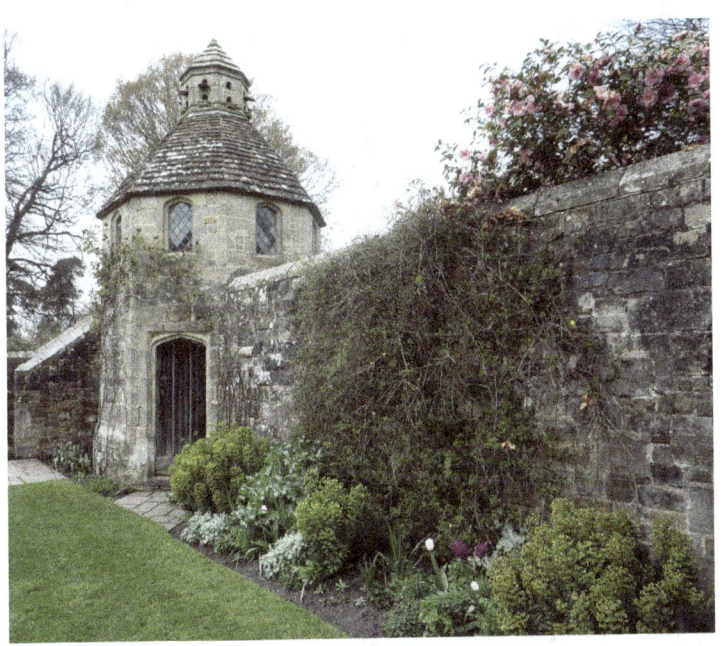

TIM SAUNDERS

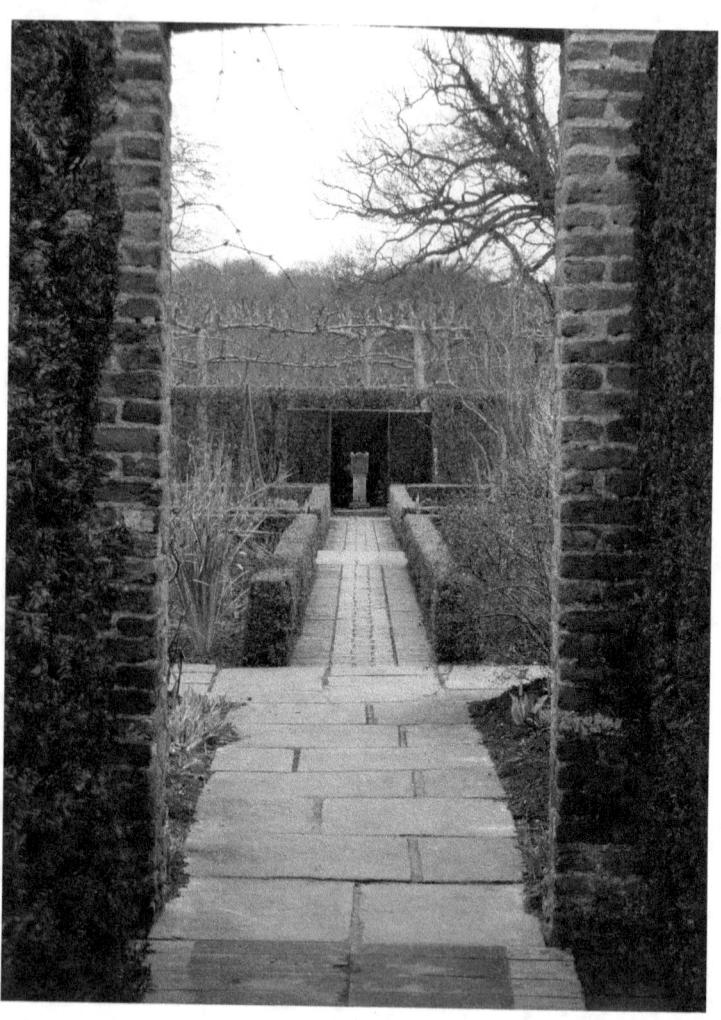

PHOTOGRAPHS OF THE BRITISH ISLES

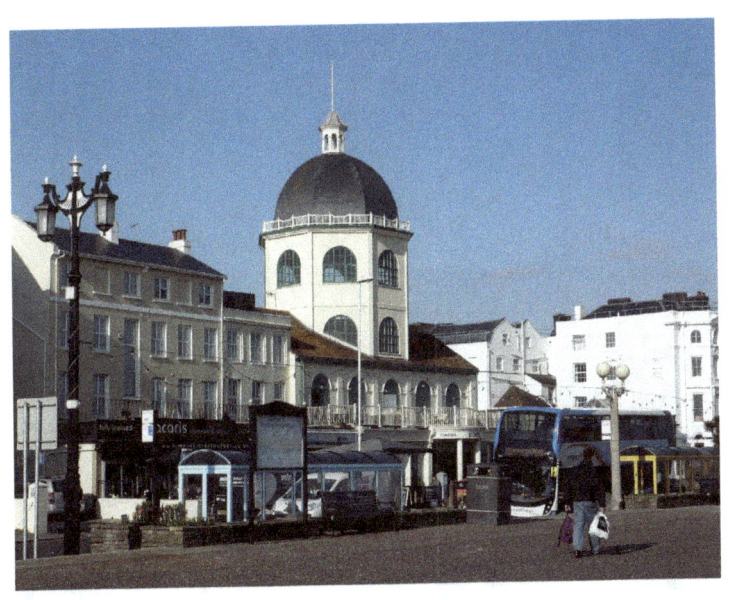

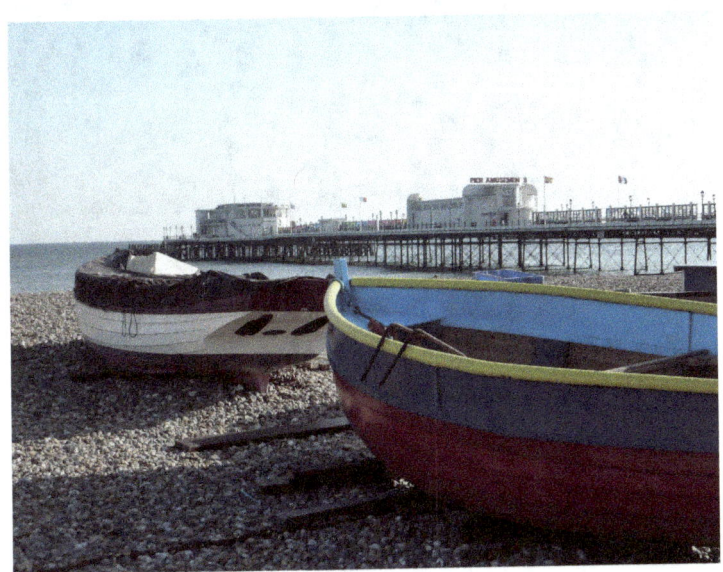

WALES

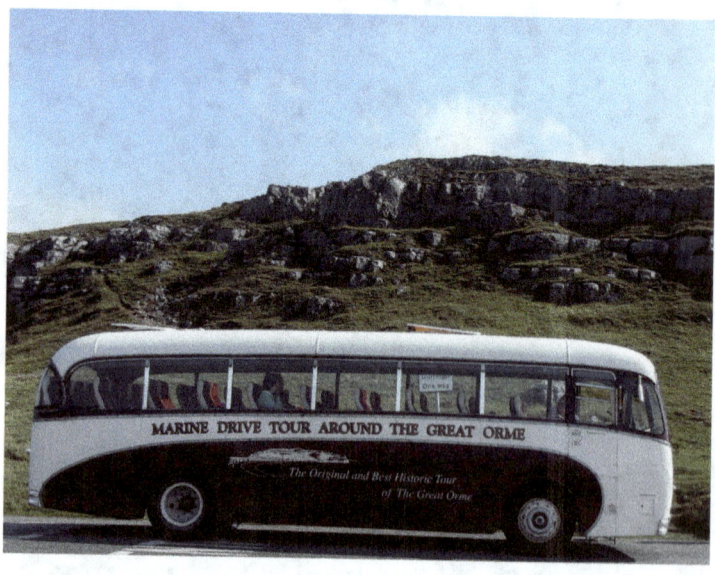

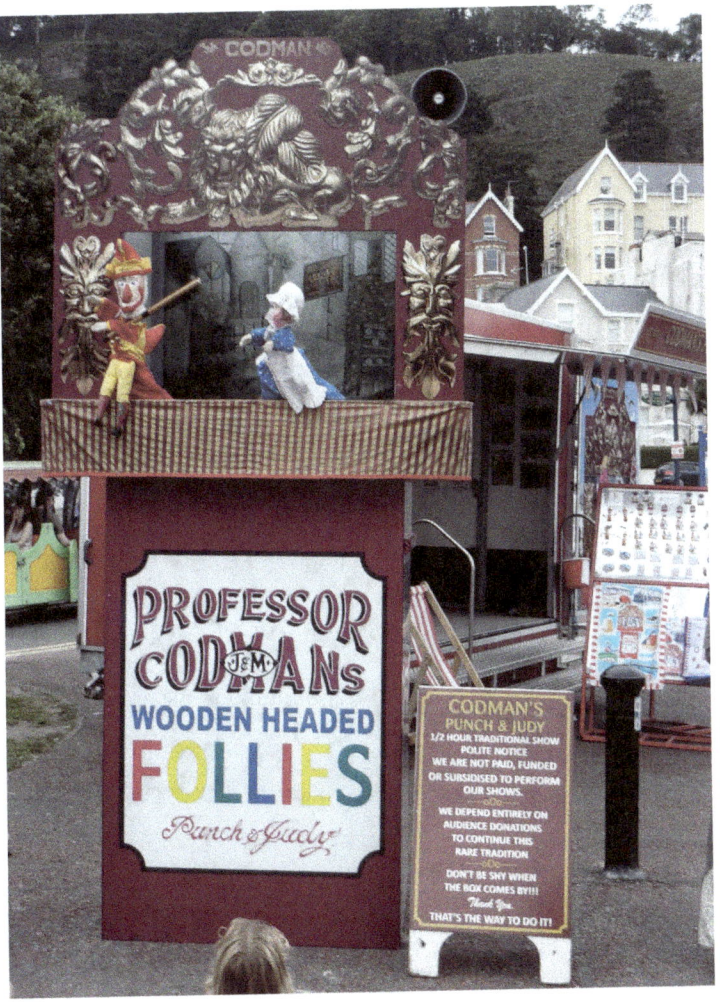

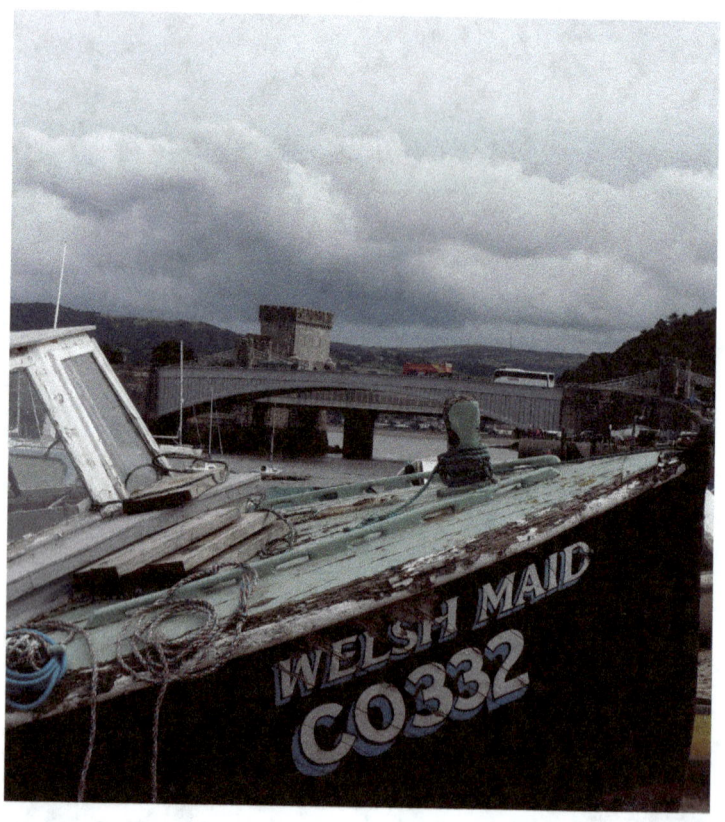

PHOTOGRAPHS OF THE BRITISH ISLES

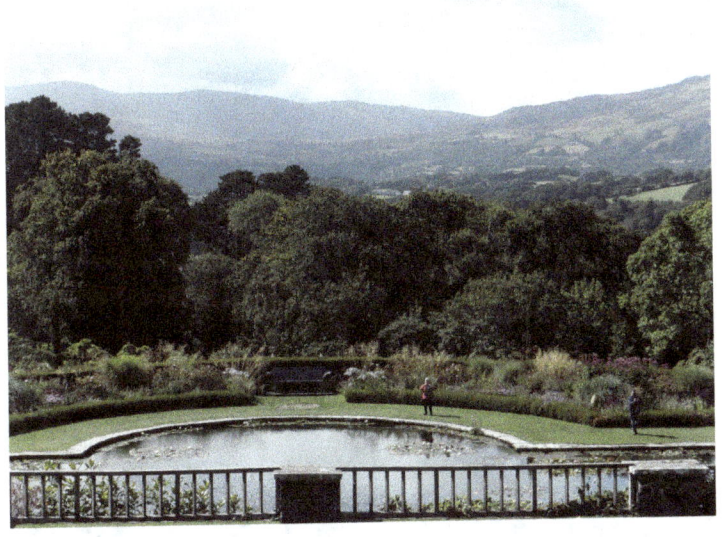

WILTSHIRE

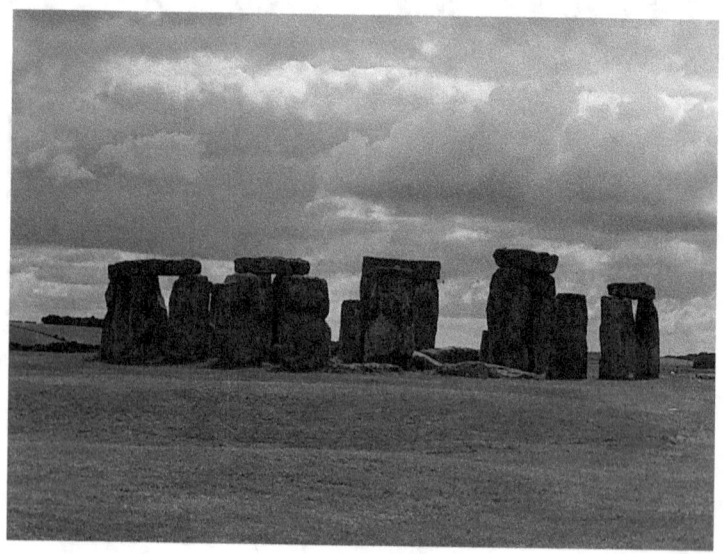

PHOTOGRAPHS OF THE BRITISH ISLES

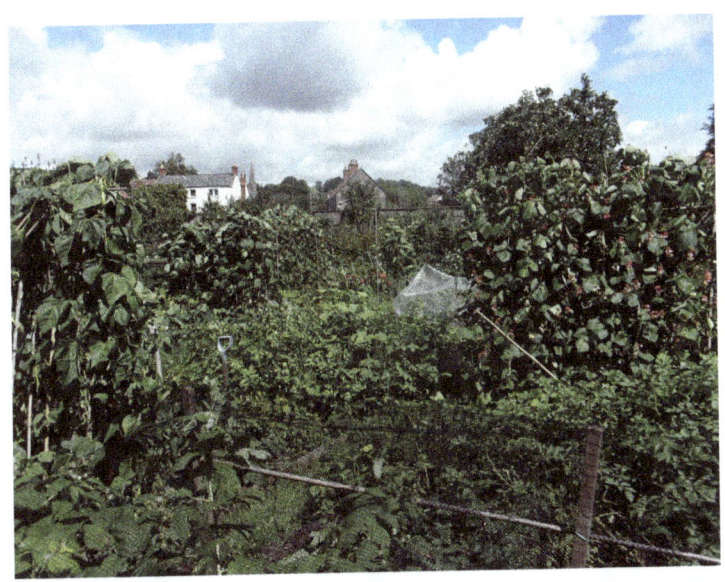

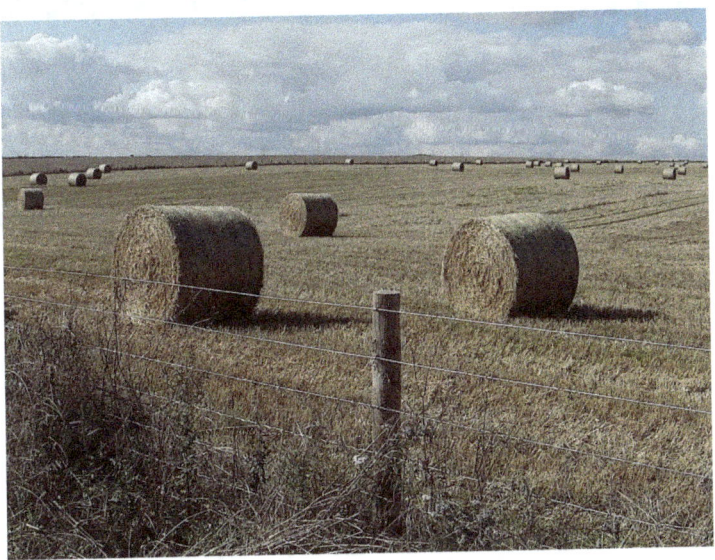

ANIMALS

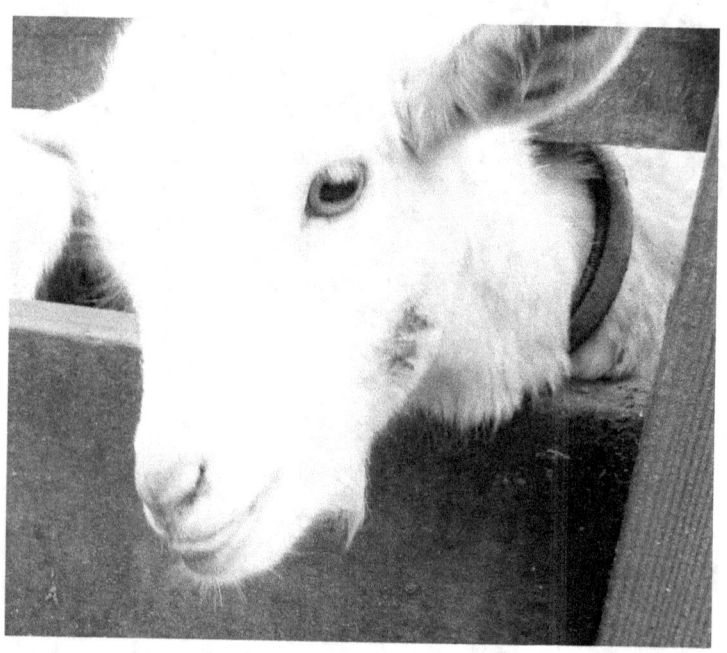

PHOTOGRAPHS OF THE BRITISH ISLES

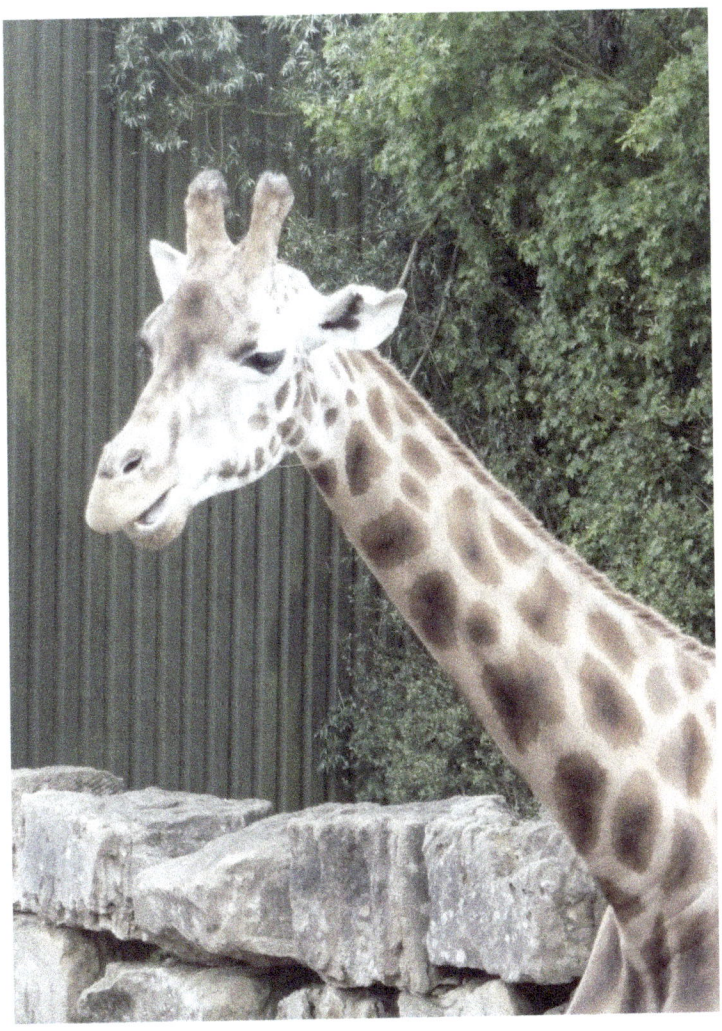

TIM SAUNDERS

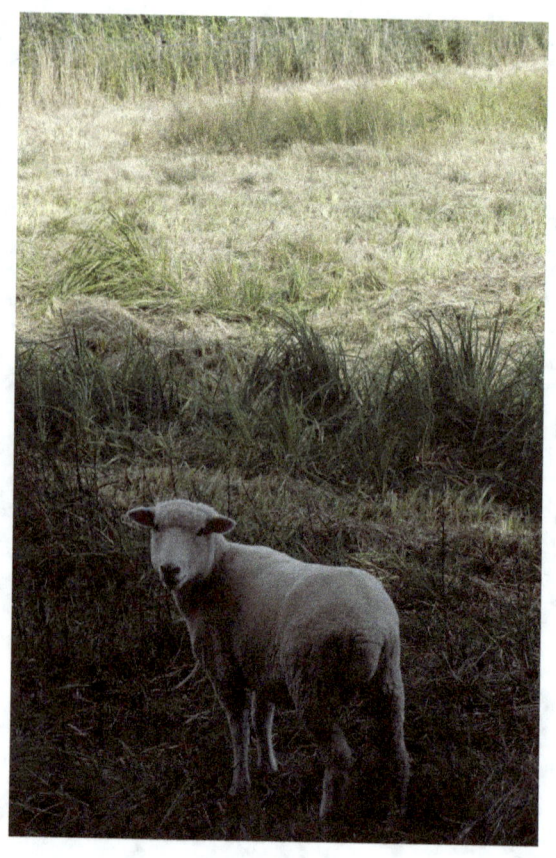

PHOTOGRAPHS OF THE BRITISH ISLES

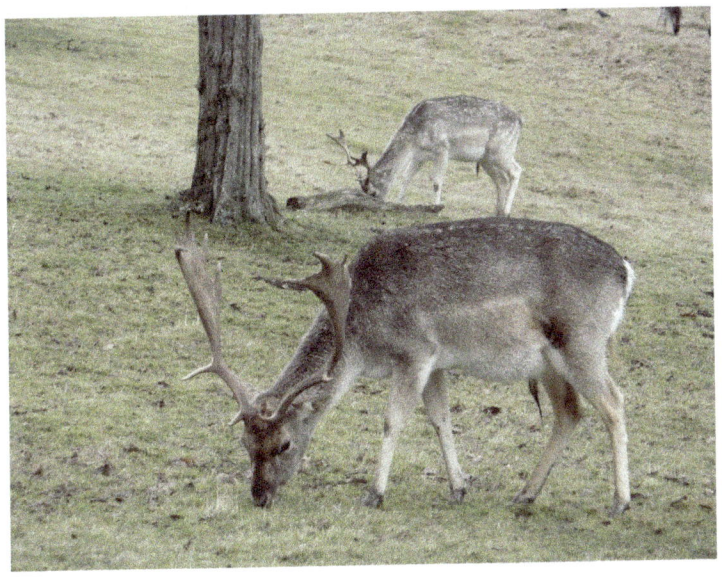

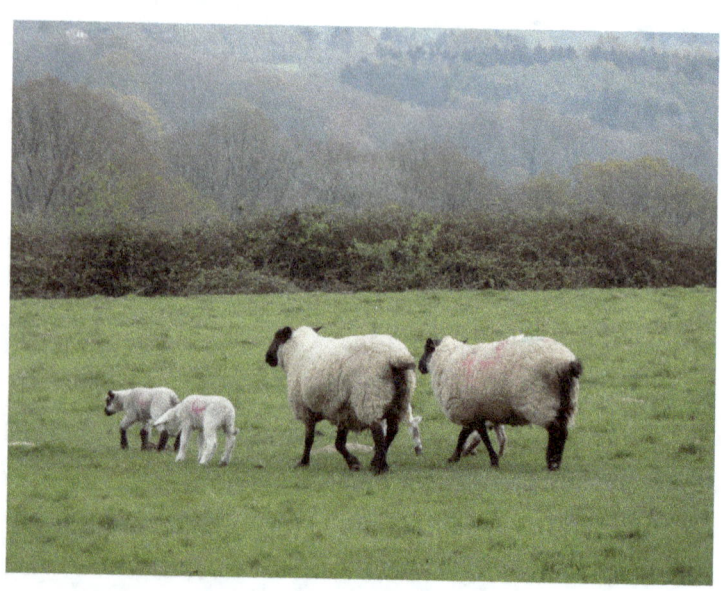

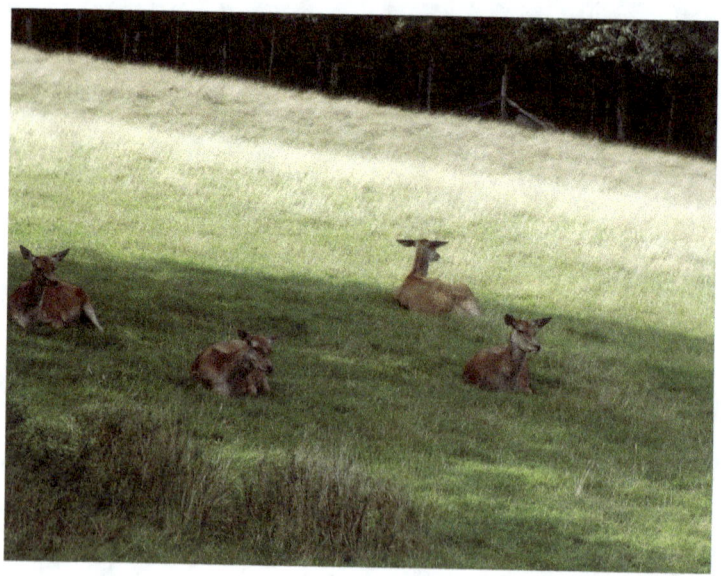

BIRDS

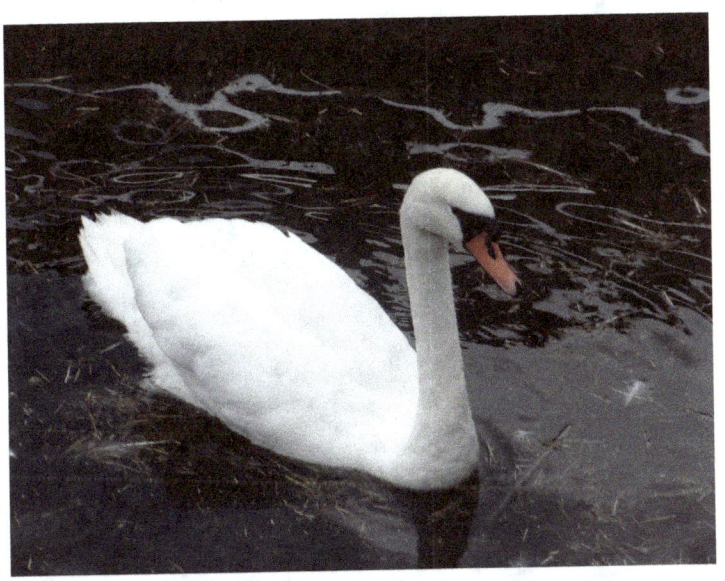

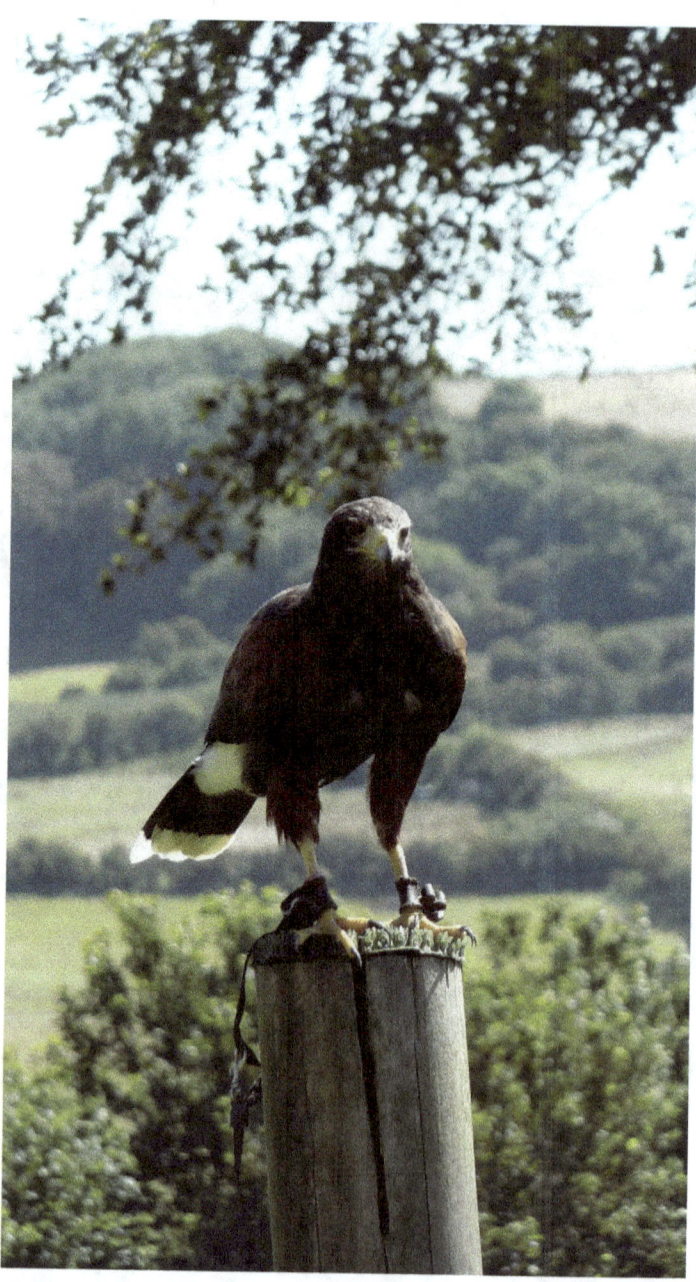

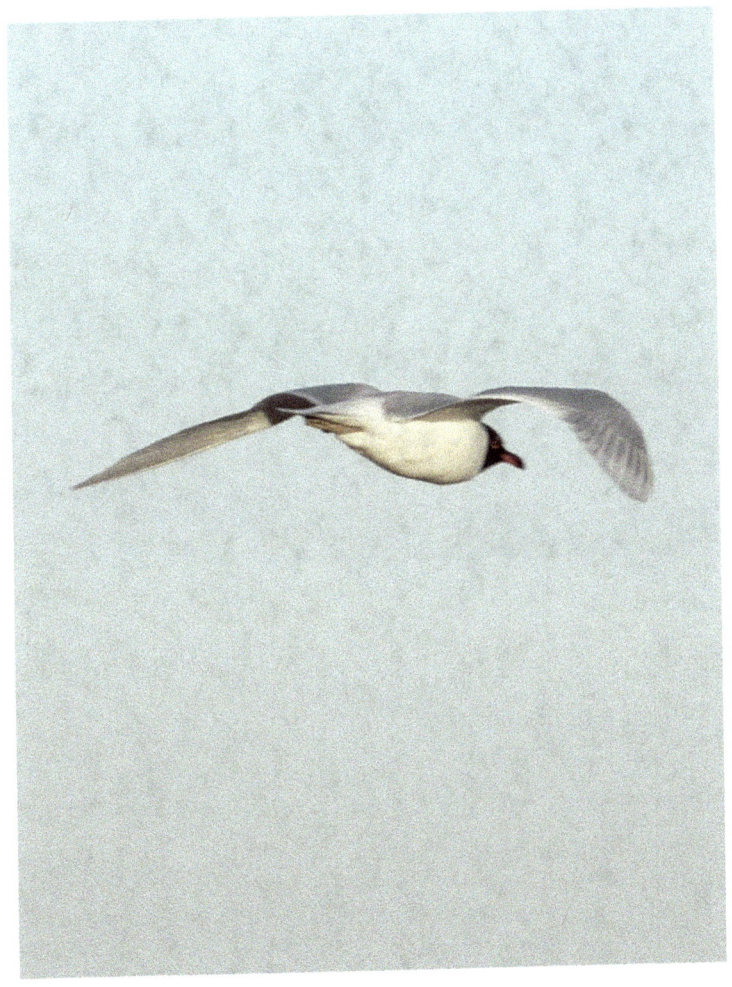

TIM SAUNDERS

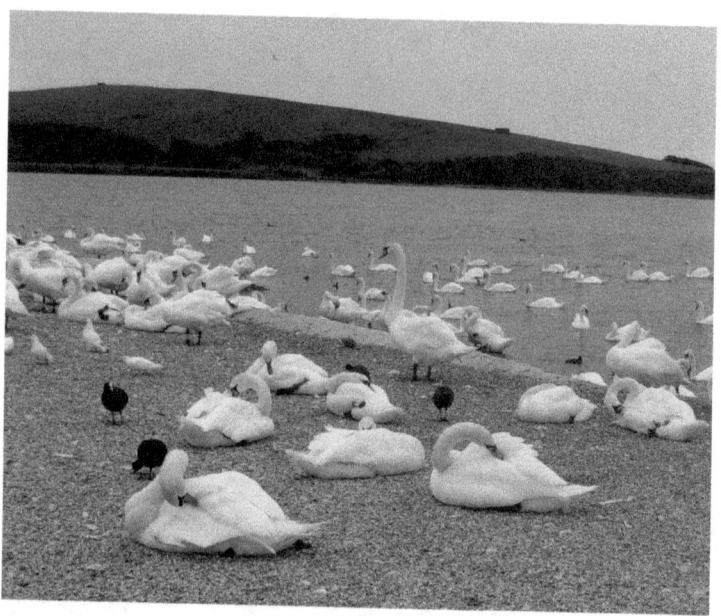

FLOWERS
and insects...

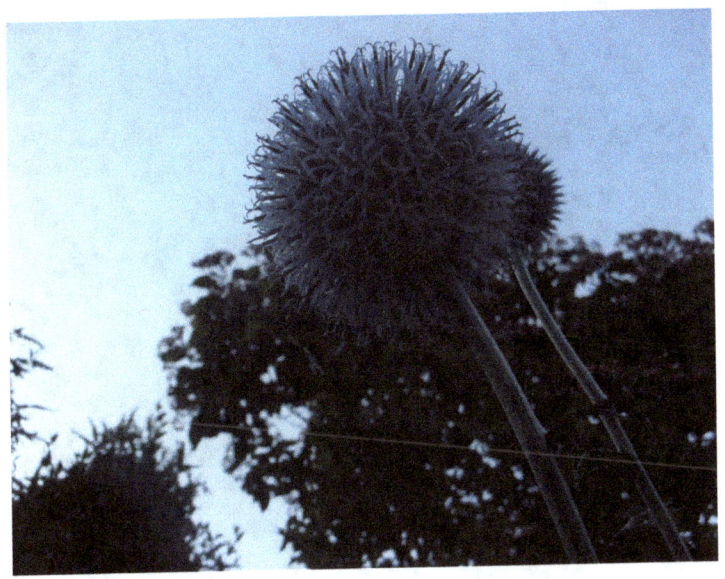

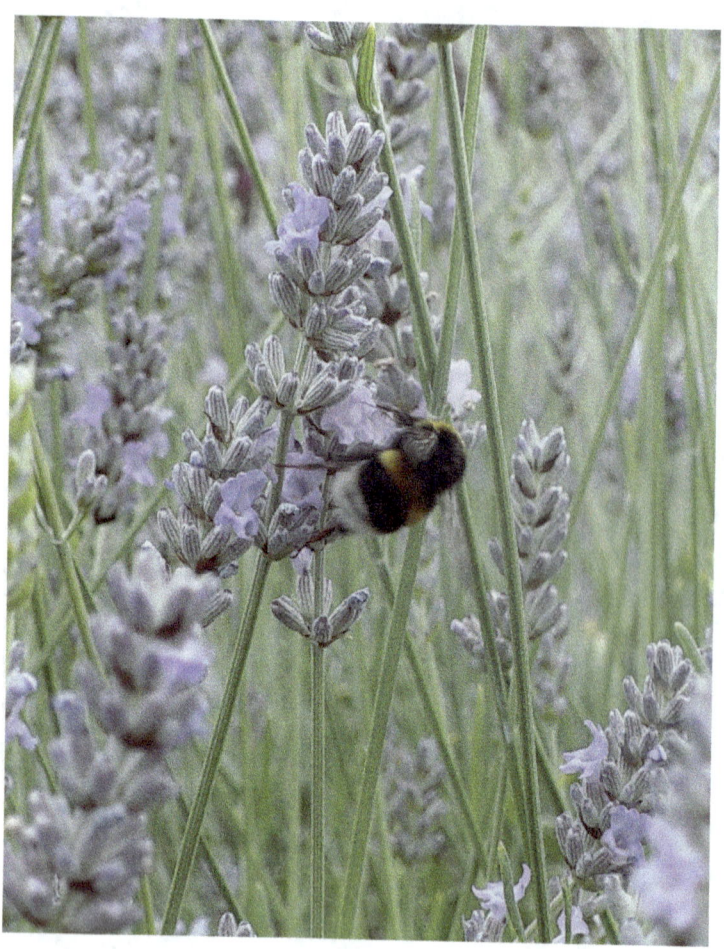

PHOTOGRAPHS OF THE BRITISH ISLES

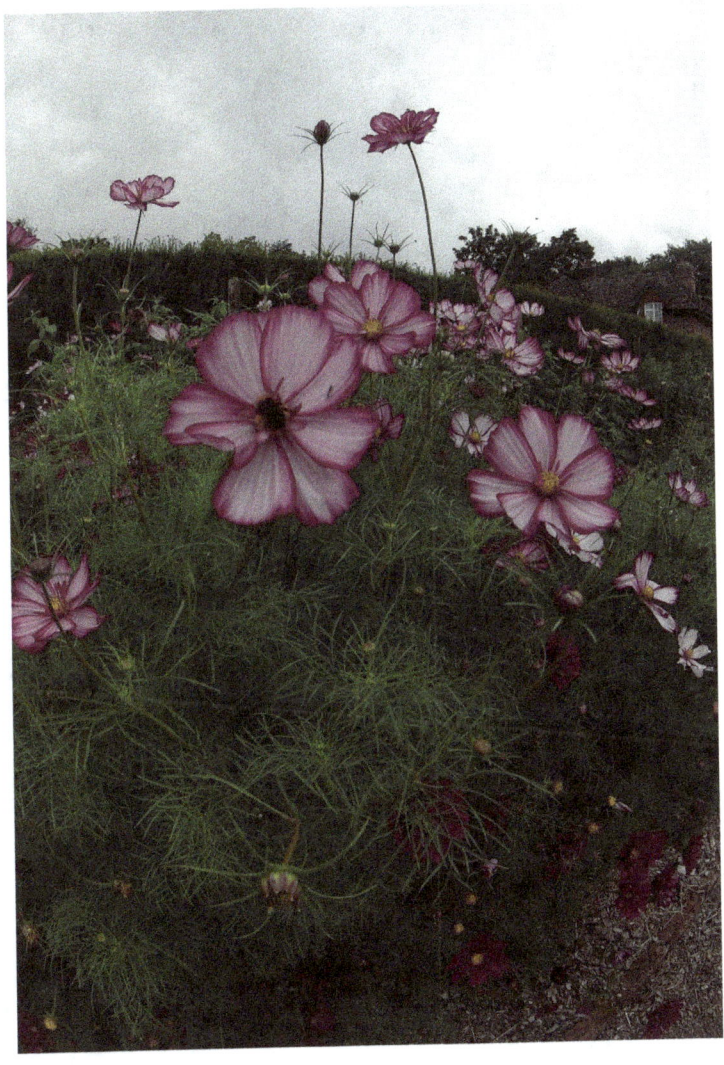

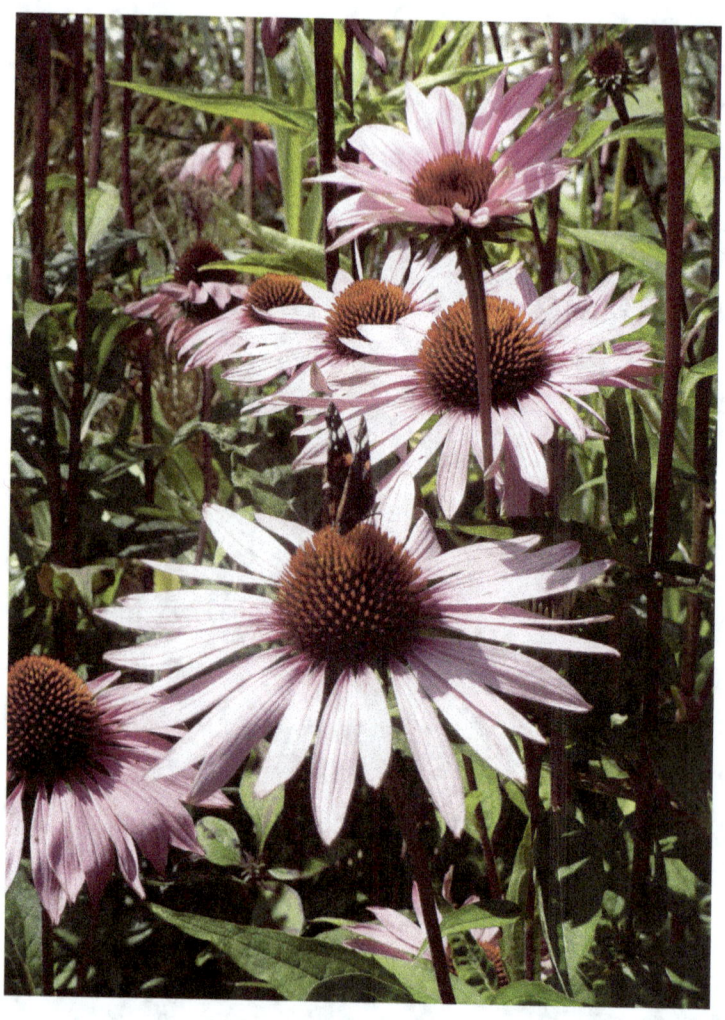

PHOTOGRAPHS OF THE BRITISH ISLES

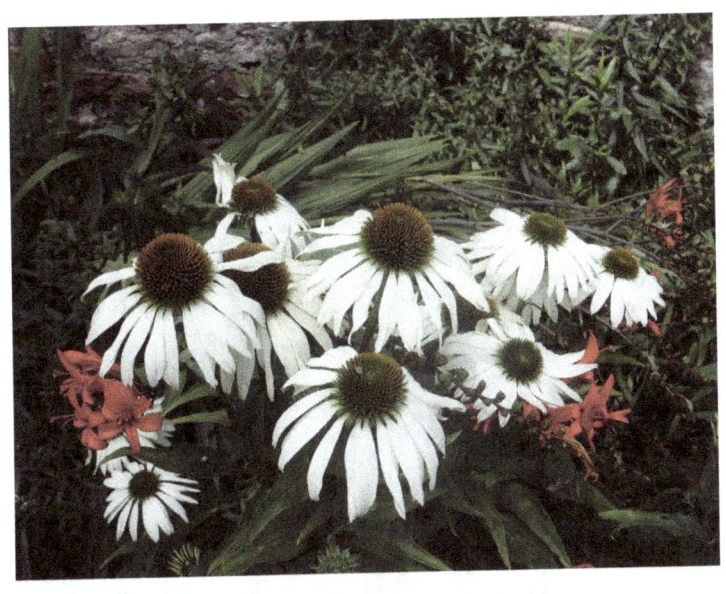

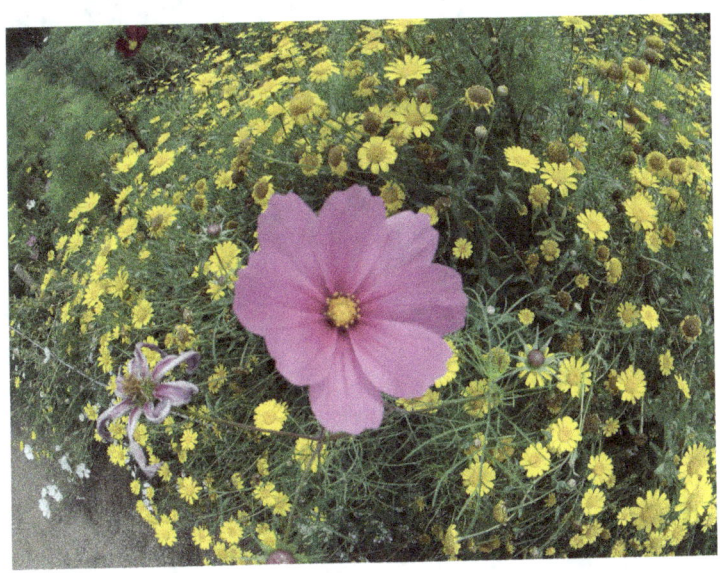

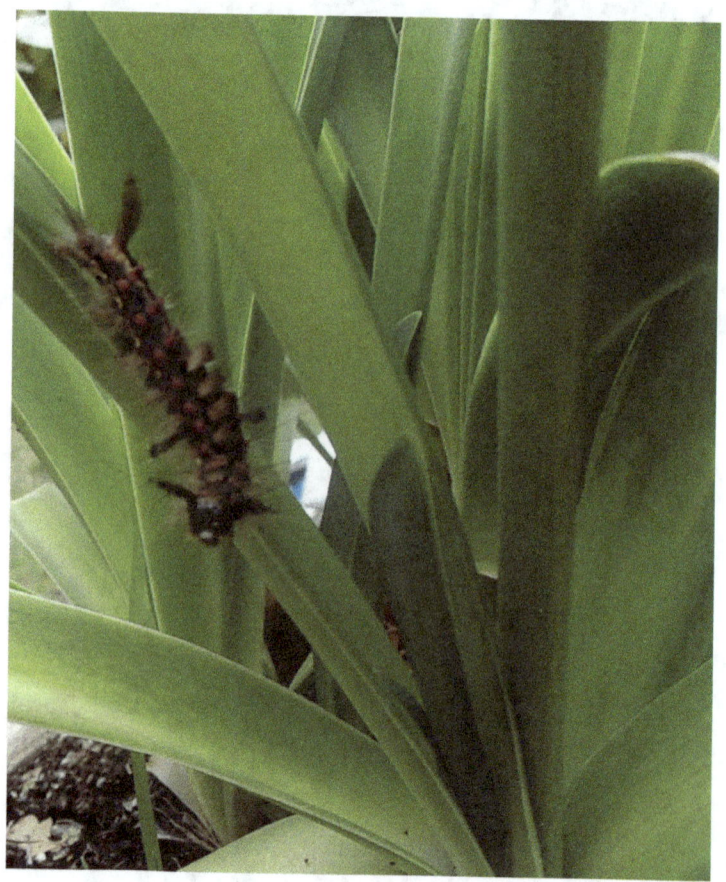

PHOTOGRAPHS OF THE BRITISH ISLES

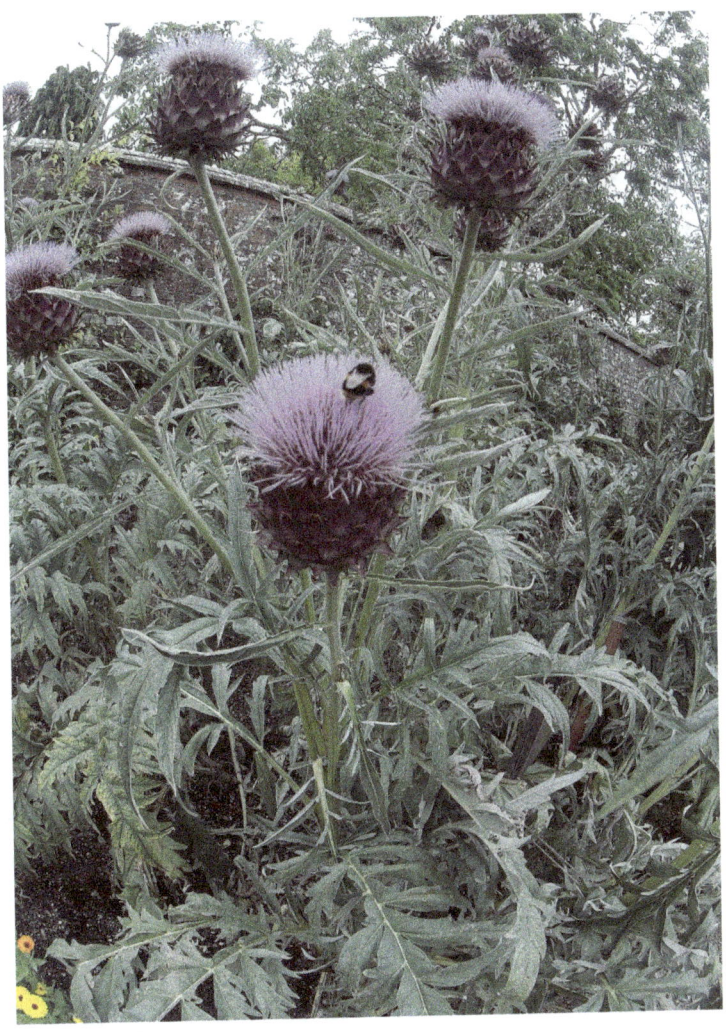

LIMITED EDITION PRINTS

Many of the photographs available in this book are available as limited edition prints from the Tim Saunders gallery:

www.artfinder.com/artist/tim-saunders

TIM SAUNDERS PUBLICATIONS
publishers of poetry, fiction and memoir

"Everybody has a book in them,"
*according to journalist
Christopher Hitchens (1949 to 2011)*

Do you have a book you would like to publish?

Email. tsaunderspubs@gmail.com
For more information visit:
tsaunderspubs.weebly.com